BEST CONTEMPORARY MONOLOGUES FOR MEN 18–35

BEST CONTEMPORARY MONOLOGUES FOR MEN 18–35

EDITED BY LAWRENCE HARBISON

APPLAUSE
THEATRE & CINEMA BOOKS
An Imprint of Hal Leonard Corporation

Published in 2014 by Applause Theatre & Cinema Books
An Imprint of Hal Leonard Corporation
7777 West Bluemound Road
Milwaukee, WI 53213

Trade Book Division Editorial Offices
33 Plymouth St., Montclair, NJ 07042

Permissions can be found on page 193, which constitutes
an extension of this copyright page.

Printed in the United States of America

Book design by John J. Flannery

Library of Congress Cataloging-in-Publication Data

Best contemporary monologues for men 18-35 / edited by
Lawrence Harbison.
     pages cm
 ISBN 978-1-4803-6961-0 (pbk.)
 1. Monologues. 2. Acting--Auditions. 3. Men--Drama. I.
Harbison, Lawrence, editor.
 PN2080.B415 2014
 812'.6--dc23
                          2014012575

www.applausebooks.com

CONTENTS

INTRODUCTION

Here you will find 101 terrific monologues for men, all from recent plays. Most have a present-tense dramatic action, because I believe that these are the most effective, whether in class or for auditions. In the cases where I have included a story monologue, though, it was a great story. Some are comic (laughs), some are dramatic (generally, no laughs). Some are rather short, some are rather long.

Several of the monologues are by playwrights whose work may be familiar to you—writers such as Don Nigro, Itamar Moses, Terrence Mc-Nally, Stephen Adly Guirgis, Charles Fuller, Adam Rapp, and Emily Mann. Other monologues are by exciting up-and-comers such as Nicole Pandolfo, C.S. Hanson, Kimberly Pau, J. Thalia Cunningham, Rachel Bonds, Rod MacLachlan, Greg Kalleres, Chad Beckim, Lucas Hnath, Merridith Allen, Reina Hardy, and Dominique Morisseau. All represent the best in contemporary playwriting.

Many of the plays from which these monologues have been culled have been published previously and, hence, are readily available either from the publisher/licensor or from a theatrical bookstore such as the Drama Book Shop in New York. A few of the plays might not be published for a while, in which case you can contact the author or his or her agent to request a copy of the entire text of the play that contains the monologue that suits your fancy. Information on publishers/rights holders may be found in the Play Sources and Acknowledgments section in the back of this anthology.

Break a leg at that audition! Knock 'em dead in class!

Lawrence Harbison
Brooklyn, NY

BEST CONTEMPORARY MONOLOGUES FOR MEN 18–35

ABOUT SPONTANEOUS COMBUSTION
Sherry Kramer

Seriocomic
ROB, late 20s to early 30s

ROB *is an assistant district attorney—a fine, upstanding, and very frustrated young man. He is in love with* AMALIA *and she with him, but she won't sleep with him because she's scared that if they touch, or even get too close, they will explode into flames.* ROB *tries to bring his considerable legal skills to bear on the problem, listing possible causes of the irrational fear* AMALIA *has of loving him.*

ROB   Let's face facts, Amalia. If you're not afraid of me because of the way I look, it follows that you do not love me for the way I look. That's assuming a cause-and-effect relationship between love, fear, and spontaneous combustion. Because there's a certain beauty about being loved for your looks. A certain . . . certainty. If someone loves you for your looks, chances are they are not going to change their mind. How could they change their mind about your looks? You look the way you look. They either love you for it or they don't. And your looks are something you can be sure of, because . . . they are a self-evident fact, anybody can see them, you can see them, too. The further beauty of this system is that if you loved me for my looks but there was this one particular part, or two parts, even, of my looks you didn't love—say these were the parts that frightened you—I could, without too much trouble, change them. If you loved me for my looks, I'd be crazy not to. But if you don't love me for my looks, I don't know where to start. There is a limit, a range, a—certainty—to the sound of my voice, in the color of my eyes. If you loved me for that particular sound, that shade of color—I'd be safe, secure. But there's no telling what the

1

rest of me—if it's the rest of me you love—can do. If it's something inside me—something I can never see and can never know—how will I identify it? How will I ever be able to make it go away? And if what has got you frightened is also what you love—then why should I?

AEROSOL DREAMS
Nicole Pandolfo

Seriocomic
TOMMY, 20s

TOMMY *tends bar at a go-go joint in New Jersey. He is talking to*
B.J., *a local cop, who has observed that some of the women in the
bar have been eyeing* TOMMY. TOMMY *is not interested in them,
which amazes* B.J.

TOMMY   I've banged so many hot chicks it's ridiculous. I used
to be in a band. MTV2 played our music video like on the
hour the whole month of March 2009. We filmed the video
ourselves. We did a major tour of New England. Played
shows all up in Boston, Providence; even hit up some spots
in Connecticut and Long Island. The Jersey Shore scene like
mad. Then we started getting the Lower East Side spots,
and then we started to really hit people's radar.

[*He reminisces a moment.*]

That was so fucking awesome. Riding the wave of like,
imminent success. One of the greatest feelings I've ever
had. I scored so many chicks. So many hot chicks. Mostly
NYU chicks in the city, but they're kinda worldly, you know,
harder to impress. The chicks in New England, it was like,
these chicks were dying for a taste of something bigger
than what they could get at their local Stop and Shop, and
to be banging a future potential rock star just set them off
like a firecracker. I haven't gotten blown with that much
enthusiasm since I was fifteen. [*Beat.*] We were . . . we were
so close. Came really close to getting a gig with EMI, Sony,
Capitol. [*Beat.*] But fucking Darin. The lead singer. He just,
he just couldn't not be a dick. It was like, he felt like finally,

he was getting the recognition that was owed to him or some shit—so instead of being grateful for the opportunities, he was more like, "fuck all of you for taking so long to notice." [*Beat.*] So he dicked around with Sony; free drinks, free food, and then it was "more money or fuck you." Same story with EMI and Capitol and even some smaller labels. And pretty soon our one video got old, our manager dropped us, and no one was left to finance any new songs or set up any new gigs. [*Beat.*] And here I am, not playing with a band, tending bar for what will be the third year in a row. So if you wonder why I don't go ape over all the hot chicks in the bar, it's because I've fucked all the hot chicks already. And they liked me better when I was a rock star.

AFTER
Chad Beckim

Dramatic
WARREN: early 30s, American-Indian

WARREN *works at a doggy day care. He is talking to* MONTY, *who has just gotten out of prison, exonerated for a crime he didn't do.* MONTY *is applying for a job.*

WARREN   My father really is the destroyer of lives, though. That was his nickname for himself when I was a child. I got this record—Shamu and Friends—for my birthday one year? It was all of the characters from SeaWorld singing songs about the sea and about the environment. That was my shit, man—I played it over and over. And one day, my father came home in a bad mood, and I was playing it in my room and he came in and said, "Turn it down." And he closed my door, and I did, and then a few minutes later he came back in and said it again, "Turn it down." And even though I already did. And a few minutes later he came back in and grabbed the record and said, "I told you to turn that fucking thing down!" and threw it against the wall and it shattered into a million pieces. And I cried and my mother came in and was like, "Why didn't you just turn it down?" even though I did. And I wouldn't talk to him for a week, and finally a week later my mom came home with a new record and hands it to me, and it's Sigmund the Sea Monster, which is not even nearly the same thing, and she's like, "This is from your father and me." And when I told her that it wasn't the same one, my father laughed and said, "I'm the destroyer of lives." Because he is.

AFTER
Chad Beckim

Dramatic
MONTY: mid-30s, Latino

MONTY *has recently been released from prison, exonerated after serving 17 years for a rape he didn't commit. He has just heard the news that his beloved dog, Ripley, was hit by a car and killed, and expresses his grief to the bearer of this bad news, CHAP, his friend and former counselor, who has also told him that he is to receive a payment of reparations from the state. LAURA MILLER is the woman whose testimony sent him to prison, who has been trying to contact him since he has been released.*

MONTY   Ripley was a good dog, man. A good dog. No, a great fucking dog. The best. I taught her to sit. I taught her to stay. I taught her to lie down. I taught her to shake—even though I wasn't supposed to. I taught her to nudge someone's hand when they were scared or angry or anxious or just, just shut the fuck down. Me. I did that. The first night in that place with me, she cried. She fucking whined, man. Just scared. Cold and dark and metal and concrete and fucking . . . hell, man. Fucking hell. And because I was used to it, I had to make her okay. And I got down on the floor with her, on her bed, and laid down next to her, and I talked to her all night and stroked her head—that was her favorite—the top of her head—and took care of her. I made her not afraid. I made her okay. I did that. I got her through hell and I made something good happen. One good thing that I did. And now it's like everything else. Gone, man. It's all gone. I have nothing. [*A long beat.*] Laura Miller can suck my dick. Fuck that bitch, man. Fuck her. The state can suck my dick. $250,000? $10 mil? What's the fucking difference, man? I am seventeen years old. Seven-fucking-teen. I don't know how to tie a tie. I don't know how to shop for toothbrushes or deodorant or toilet paper. I don't know how to use a computer. I don't know how to kiss. My dick doesn't work. I can't help my friend, I can't protect a woman. I cannot do anything anything—ANYTHING—without being told to. The only fucking good thing I ever did is gone, and you come here telling me that the good news is that they want to pay me for missing my prom and college and keg parties and my first apartment? Fuck them. Fuck the dude that killed my dog. And fuck Laura Miller.

AMERICAN DUET
Mark Leib

Dramatic
CHARLIE, 23

CHARLIE *is talking to* JESSICA, *the young woman he loves.*
CHARLIE, *who until recently has not been interested in politics, has
started working for the Jimmy Carter presidential campaign, because* JESSICA *has informed him that she can't love a man who's
not engaged politically. The fact that* JESSICA *is married and has
told him that she is not interested in being involved romantically
with him hasn't daunted him one bit.*

CHARLIE   Look, Andrea and I went to see *Rocky* a few days
   ago. Have you seen it? Well, this is the story of a loser, a
   nobody, a washed-out case who gets a shot at the heavy-
   weight title, and a chance to redeem all the humiliations
   he's suffered his entire life. And I'm sitting there in the
   movie theater, and I'm thinking, I identify with him. Me,
   from an upper-middle-class home, and I can't help but see
   myself in Rocky Balboa. Because I was supposed to get
   lost in the shuffle, just like him. My parents expected me
   to become an attorney like every other kid I knew, and just
   like them I was supposed to make an enormous amount of
   money, and just like them I was supposed to stay high on
   steak dinners and vacations to the South of France, and I
   was to die a rich and happy nobody, totally detached from
   any issue that mattered more than the relative comforts
   of a Mercedes and a BMW. And I was moving along fine on
   this pleasant trajectory, and I took one small detour: I fell in
   love with you. And you said to me something, you said you
   knew in your heart that one day I was going to involve myself in the world. That I was going to notice it, the politics

and the history and the suffering too. And I made a start—I wrote a thesis about an event that we both lived through but that I really didn't understand. And then that wasn't enough, so I signed up with this campaign, which I just knew you'd approve. And now I don't know what's next, but I've taken steps, and I'm sure that others will follow. My life's going to matter, and not just to my stockbroker. That's what you've done to me. [*Pause*.] I don't want to stop working with you. You've changed me. You're still changing me.

APOSIOPESIS
John P. McEneny

Seriocomic
MARCEL, 23

On the Quad on a brisk fall afternoon, a frazzled young man is being followed by a small, stern girl, BETH LOOPER, *23, a brilliant student at Saddlewood College. She has romantic feelings for her friend,* MARCEL STANICIU, *23. They are romantic literature majors. Here, he confronts her and sets her straight.*

MARCEL   Lower your voice. I was not playing with Elina Plugaru's ponytail during the lecture. I was not stroking it. I was barely petting it. It was just there. Dangling freely on my desk while I'm taking notes. What the hell am I supposed to do? Who are you to judge me? Why are you even watching me? Beth!? Beth. NO! NO! What do you even care what I do with Elina Plugaru's hair? You're not my girlfriend. You had your chance one year ago at Model Congress and you blew it, lady! And don't pretend you were drunk on wine coolers, because the stuff you said was really cruel and small and unforgiveable. And it wasn't a perm—it was a relaxer. Many men use it. I told you—my cousin Manny mixed the ammonium thioglycolate with too much petroleum jelly and then left it in too long . . . and he should have used a neutralizer and just shut up. NO! Maybe I was just trying to look nice for you. [*Pause.*] That night at the Comfort Inn was really important to me. It was supposed to have been special and it took a lot of planning on my part. I was very vulnerable and you knew it. It may not have been your first time but it was mine and I wanted it to be nice. And you ruined it. I had to borrow money from my dad. I had to pay almost three hundred dollars for a new ozonator because the rose petals got stuck in the filter of the Jacuzzi. I had to borrow money from my dad. Try lying to your dad that you were at a Comfort Inn ALONE on a Tuesday night in a Jacuzzi filled with rose petals. He still won't look at me. It doesn't matter anymore. I'm happy now. Now finally I'm happy and I don't think about you anymore. I feel good about myself, and my hair is growing in, and I'm happy, and I aced my GRE's and now . . . NOW, you're acting like a scorned woman? Like you're Nastasya Filippovna from that stupid Dostoyevsky novel. If you think you're going to bring your jealousy and misplaced romantic aspirations into a literary journal, then you're dead wrong. You're not ruining my senior year, Beth.

BABY PLAYS THE BANJO
Kimberly Pau

Dramatic
ROB, 30

Speaking to the audience, ROB *is defending the inappropriate relationship he has with his colleague's daughter, who is 24 but acts much younger and is emotionally challenged.*

ROB   You know about me? How I used to be? Well, you'd hear it around Syosset. If you kept your ears open, you'd hear what they're saying about me. So what? I don't give a shit. I built that bike, you know. Piece by piece. I bought the parts. I selected each one separately for quality. And I put it together. And it works and it gets me where I need to go. And I'm like a car but I'm the engine you know. I made the parts. The flesh and the steel and it all passed through my hands and I deserve some fucking respect for that shit. I don't get it. I'm not gonna be pushed around. No one is pushing me around. There is nothing soft. Nothing quiet about me, nothing small about me. You can't blame me. I don't know when the things I wanted became so hard. My parents, they had a little house and some kids. They had a boat and a truck and a basketball net and camping on vacation and shit. And I'm just this asshole with a camera and a bike, riding around like a clown, a clown with very good posture but nonetheless, some asshole. And I'm not trying hurt no one. I just need what you need, alright? Give me a break! Just let me keep going. You don't see my plan okay. You don't see where this is heading. It's going somewhere it's all gonna be clear and no one's gonna be mad about any of it when they figure it out. Because I see far into the future. Baby, I see what none of you seen yet. I see where we're going cuz I've been there and I'm going back bigger. And I'm taking what's mine this time. I'm not getting kicked around by nobody. I'm catching it all on tape. I got it locked down. Don't worry about it. You're gonna understand. You'll get it when we get there. You'll see.

THE BAD GUYS
Alena Smith

Dramatic
JESSE, 20s

JESSE has dropped by to visit his old friend NOAH *before* NOAH *heads out to Los Angeles to pursue his dream of becoming a filmmaker. Here, he rants to* NOAH *and others in the backyard of* NOAH's *mom's house.*

JESSE   Fuckin' Chris. Thinks he's so great 'cause he's going back to school. Well, you know what that means? Debt. More debt. Chris and April are gonna be in debt for the rest of their lives, and so is their kid. And so are my parents. I'm the only one with my head above water, and that's because I sell ganja to children. But of course, that's a Band-Aid solution. Ultimately, I'm fucked too. This whole country's fucked, you know that? Thanks to people like Fink. You know Fink was the one who kept telling my dad to build those shitty spec houses! Oh, everyone's doing it. Easy money. Get in on the game, Glen. 'Cause houses aren't for living in anymore. They're for flipping! Like burgers. But then the big burger bubble blows up. And who do you think gets bailed out? Not us, nah. We go broke.

Fink and his buddies—*they're* the ones getting government cheese. Welfare for Wall Street, that's what America is all about. Ain't that ironic? Dontcha think? 'Cause America, we hate welfare! Like when I see fat bitches with babies hanging off their tits lining up for a handout—that just makes me *sick*. As an *American*, that just makes me puke a little bit in my mouth. But now Fink and his friends, they're special. They're too big to fail! So these guys, these banksters, what they need from us—what they need from *you*, America—is, oh, just a little thing called seven hundred billion dollars. Oh—and that's just to start. An appetizer—no, an appe-teaser. That's what they call it at Applebee's, right? And you know what they call it at KFC. [*Beat.*] A Double Down. Yup. That's what we did here, America. We just doubled the fuck *down* on this bullshit.

BARBARY FOX
Don Nigro

Seriocomic
BERT, 29

BARBARY FOX *is a beautiful orphan, raised at the dump by her strange uncle* REM, *who locks her in the fruit cellar every night to keep the boys away from her.* BERT *is an occasionally charming but somewhat dangerous young man with a murky past who has appeared in town and possibly blackmailed his friend* SILAS *into giving him a good job at the cheese factory and a nice house next door to his, and now he wants* BARBARY *to marry him. She protests that they don't know each other and that people will think he's crazy to marry a girl from the dump who everybody believes is the town slut. Here, he deftly cuts his way through all her protests.*

BERT   Barbary, you're making this way too complicated. This is a very simple thing. Here's the deal. Do you want out of the mess you're in, up here by the dump and the fireworks factory and the chicken-plucking plant, or don't you? Because I've got a brand-new house at 413 Armitage Avenue, right next to my good friend Silas Quiller's place, and a good job managing his cheese factory, and a lifetime pass to his gazebo, and I'm absolutely prepared to make you my lawfully wedded wife this very night, preacher and papers and everything, and you'll never have to go back to that fruit cellar again. Knowledge is highly overrated. Nobody knows anybody. Why waste six months pretending to get to know each other when at the end of it we'll be more ignorant about who we are than we were to begin with? You marry me and thirty years from now we still won't know each other. We might as well enjoy ourselves before we're old and ugly. Well, before you're old and ugly. I'm already ugly.

But I'm not as old as I will be next week. So let's get married tonight, before I get older and you get ugly. You can see what a romantic kind of a guy I am, so what do you say? People don't think much of me now. I don't give a rat's ass what people think. I don't actually like people much. Most of them are stupid and the rest are evil or crazy, and a surprising number of them are all three at the same time. Just figure out what you want, then do whatever you got to do to get it, then grab onto it and don't let go. That's all there is. Anybody says different is a liar or a fool or both. Anybody don't like it, screw 'em. Now, you want to marry me or not? What's the matter? You want to get out of that place, I give you what you want, and you're too scared to take it? You want to spend the rest of your life getting locked up in the fruit cellar? Is that how it is? You like that fruit cellar? You feel safe there? Because let me tell you, sweetheart. Nothing is safe. No place, no person, nothing. And there ain't no cuddles in the grave. You want to be alive for a while before God kills you, or what?

BETHANY
Laura Marks

Dramatic
GARY, 20s to 30s

GARY *is a squatter who lives in foreclosed houses, staying in one house until the bank auctions it, and then moving on to the next one. He is somewhat demented, possibly dangerous. He is talking to* CRYSTAL, *who lost her house and is now staying in another foreclosed house while she tries to get her life back together. She wound up in a shelter and lost custody of her 5-year-old daughter,* BETHANY. GARY *wants* CRYSTAL *to fight back.*

GARY   They're socializing her. They're teaching her not to hit other kids, and to keep her skirt down, and raise her hand when she has to go to the bathroom. Every single thing her body wants to do is getting smashed down by the military-industrial complex, and the worst part is that it happens all day, every day, to everyone, and everyone just lets it happen. Look at you: you go around all day with that big, fake smile pasted across your face, selling people a bunch of crap they don't need so you can go buy crap *you* don't need. "I just *have* to make this sale." You completely bought the government messages. But what happens now? Are you gonna just curl up and die? Or are you gonna fight back? Because when you have to struggle for food and shelter, just like we did millions of years ago, boom! You start getting your mind back. And we have to take advantage of this time and fight the system until we obliterate it. You and me, we'll never recover a hundred percent; but your daughter's young—she might still have a chance . . . You see, it won't be a collective society anymore where technology controls the masses. It'll just be individuals and small groups. And when the centers of technology and finance go down, we need to be ready to survive. Small, nomadic groups have the best shot at it. I know how to trap food and I know all the edible plants. I'll tell you what you should do. You pick her up from school. You say, "Don't worry, honey, we're never going back there again." Then the three of us get in your car and we start driving. We drive until we hit wilderness. Someplace without all this EMF radiation. We build a shelter. Or find one. And we've got the seeds of a new society.

XX . . . XX . . . XY.

BLACKTOP SKY
Christina Anderson

Dramatic
KLASS: 27, African American

*KLASS is a homeless man who lives on a bench in a housing
project. He has arranged various objects around him, to which
he addresses this monologue. KLASS evokes a performance style
similar to that of Robert Preston's when he sang "Trouble" in The
Music Man. KLASS also taps into a Baptist minister style a la Rev.
B. W. Smith. If a middle ground can be found between these two,
that'd be so so cool.*

KLASS   You may not be fully aware of the times we're livin'
in. The times that they don't print in our papers or splash
across our screens or pump through our radios. I suggest
you might not be aware, because I see you. I watch you. I
see you holding on to what little sanity and security you
have left, squeezing it so tight that the color is leaving your
fingers, draining from your hands. The squeezing is caus-
ing your muscles to ache. Jaws to clinch. And you think
that pain is a sign of sanity? Security? It's not, my friends.
It's not. [*Pause.*] There's a wind blowin' through you. [*Pause.*]
A violent gust of truth. [*Pause.*] It starts out as a breeze
somewhere in here . . . [*Points at his heart.*] . . . and it wakes
up all the noise inside of you. Then that breeze gets in your
blood. Travels through every vein. Head to toe. It gathers
enough speed to the point where it won't let you sleep
at night. That breeze becomes a gust and that gust won't
let you be still. Won't keep your troubles quiet. You sit on
stoops, lean against cars, stand under the moon—restless.
You walk to one end of your neighborhood then back to
the other end, go sit back on that same stoop, sit under the

sun—restless. The gust is stirring your soul. It's pulling up memories from way down deep, from the cracks and crevices covered with scabs and scars. We swallow what we think is liquor, inhale what we think is weed, inject what we think is freedom. We alter our state of reality so we don't have to participate in it. So we can't be responsible, aware, dependable. And what happens when we hear a scream? When we see someone who looks like us, cornered? Pleading? Hm?

[KLASS *turns away as if he's ignoring a weeping soul.*]

We cross the street. We turn the music up a little louder. We drink, smoke, squeeze . . .
but we still hear it. It never goes away. The wind, the noise, that somebody pleading . . .
it's not going away. And then the next somebody is cornered.

[KLASS *turns away.*]

And then the next one . . .

[*He turns away.*]

And then the next—until it's you. And then you want to know why no one's coming to save you, to take you to a safe place?

BROKEN FENCES
Steven Simoncic

Dramatic
HOODY: mid-30s, African American

HOODY and his fiancée, D, have lived in Garfield Park their whole lives. As the neighborhood gentrifies, their property taxes have increased and they can no longer afford to live in their own home. This is HOODY's recounting of his life and struggle for survival that continues to this very day. This monologue is delivered to the audience.

HOODY   I am invisible. Been invisible all my life. When I was a kid I could go days, weeks without being seen. Throw my hood up over my head, eyes pushed way back deep inside, and poof . . . just disappear. Blend into the street . . . another shadow . . . another shade of black and grey on the stairs by the train. [*Beat.*] Started calling me Hoody. Ain't nobody know my real name . . . and that was fine with me, 'cause I didn't need one. And I got used to it too . . . being invisible. I could flow like air, life blowing through me like a breeze. Like I wasn't there. And it was tight too 'cause when you young and you angry and you invisible, you can fuck with people and they don't even know what hit 'em. Can't catch what you can't see. And for a long time ain't nobody see me. Randolph and Kedzie, 1999. I'm standing on the corner, watchin' the Camden projects burn. Marz come running out the house all jacked up, snappin' on this light-skinned boy from Pilsen. I'm like, "Yo Marz, chill your shit"—wasn't the first time my brother's mouth got his ass in trouble—but then this light-skinned boy from Pilsen pulls out his nine mil acting all gansta and shit and—POP! POP! Busts two caps just like that. [*Beat.*] Marz ran. Didn't look back. Didn't get a scratch. Me . . . I musta been real in-visible that day 'cause that boy from Pilsen never even saw me. Bullet passed through me like a pit bull, clawing and scratching and biting its way out. Woke up in Cook County Hospital with a red Bulls jersey *that used to be white* packed into my chest. Don't even know how it got there. That was the day I became a little more . . . in focus. After a while I realized the scars weren't just on me, they *were* me. And every year, I got more. Earned every cut, every burn, every bruise, and every tattoo . . . the more marked up I got, the more I could be *seen*. 22. At least here in Garfield Park you ain't had to look hard to see me—*I was everywhere, man*—just connect my dots [*Pointing to scars on his arm.*] and you got me. [*Beat.*] Least the old me. The *fuck you* me. The *used-to-be* me. Now my shit's retired like MJ. Ham sand-wiches and double shifts, that's all I'm pulling these days. Shit I go to Costco. And I *like* it. [*Beat.*] Scars are fading . . . dots are disappearing . . . trade your bruise and tattoo for some comfortable shoes . . . and you're left with a whole lot less connect.

BROKEN FENCES

Steven Simoncic

Dramatic
SPENCE, mid-30s

SPENCER DILLAWAY *is an ad executive speaking to a group of African Americans from Garfield Park (a rough neighborhood on Chicago's deep West Side) in a focus group.* SPENCE *just a presented a new product called Cheese Chunkers—a processed cheese product with zero nutritional value that will be targeted to African American children. The people in the focus group have just called him out on this . . . and this is his defense.*

SPENCE   How many of you been to Disney World? It's real fuckin' expensive. Why? Because they sell magic. And magic ain't cheap. But just because you don't have the cash to go to Disney World doesn't mean you still don't wanna give your kids a little bit of magic . . . see that sparkle in their eyes. *They're your kids.* And that's fine, because Disney World isn't a place—it's an *idea.* It's about making your babies smile and making you feel better about being a parent. It's about aunties feeling like better aunties and uncles feeling like better uncles. *That* is its power. And that is a powerful thing. And that's exactly what *these* do. In some small, tiny way, they bring out a little bit of that magic . . . *that joy* . . . And on a snowy Wednesday in Garfield Park, when these kids *run* home from school cause they're too afraid to walk—they may be a million miles away from The Happiest Place on Earth—you can still open a box of these and—for an instant—make your kid feel special . . . and safe . . . and loved. For *five dollars and ninety-nine cents.* [*Beat.*] And if only for a moment—you *feel* better . . . 'cause things *are better.* This is affordable luxury. This is a bright spot in a long hard day. A little shot of magic in a world that desperately needs some. [*Beat.*] Now you can rag on these all you want. I'm not saying they're the end-all be-all . . . and I'm not saying to eat 'em every day . . . and I'm certainly not saying they're health food. But I am saying that there's a whole lot more in this box than cheese product. And that's what you're buying.

BRONX BOMBERS

Eric Simonson

Dramatic
REGGIE: mid-30s, African American

REGGIE JACKSON *thinks he has been unappreciated since he signed with the New York Yankees, when he announced that he was going to be "the straw that stirs the drink." His manager* BILLY MARTIN, *teammate* THURMAN MUNSON, *and Yankee great* YOGI BERRA *have been trying to get him to see himself as part of a team, part of the great Yankee Tradition, which means doing what* MARTIN *tells him to do. He responds.*

REGGIE Why?! Why do I gotta do that?! Why do I gotta do anything you tell me? But then I do. I do everything you tell me to. I ride the bus that I *hate*, I room with guys who hate *me*, I play when you say play, and I ride the bench when you say don't, even though the fans want to see me and it makes no sense whatsoever. I keep quiet—I keep quiet and I do what I'm told. And I will continue to do that all year long, and I won't ask to be traded 'cause that's what I agree to do, and thank God Almighty that I am a good, Christian, Man! That's right. Jesus! Jesus Christ got my mind right! And he hears my *suffering*! He hears my *prayers*!

[*He drops to his knees.*]

It makes me cry, the way I'm treated on this team. The Yankees are Ruth and DiMaggio and Mantle and Gehrig. I'm a nigger to you, and I just don't know how to be no Elston Howard. I'm making seven hundred thousand dollars a year, I drive a Rolls-Royce, and I got homes on both ends of this great country and you treat me like dirt. I've got an IQ of one hundred sixty, and you can't mess me because you've *never* seen anything like me, and you sure as hell never had anyone like me on the Yankees. I won't fight you, Billy Martin! I'll do whatever you tell me to do on the field, because that is my contract with you, but you can*not* make me give up on myself! You can*not* make me give up on *me*! See you at the ballpark.

CHARLES WINN SPEAKS

C.S. Hanson

Dramatic
CHARLES, mid-30s

CHARLES, *a Russian immigrant who became a Wall Street hot-shot, almost lost the woman of his dreams. In this monologue, which takes place in a hospital corridor, we realize that he not only married the woman but she has just given birth to their first child. Speaking into a smart phone,* CHARLES *records a podcast to his newborn son.*

CHARLES   This may be the only time I will get to say, I don't know, certain things. Once we leave this place, we'll be off and running. It will pass too fast. I want to hold on to time, to hold on to you. And so I make this podcast—for you and you alone. I speak to you while I can, before you are climbing the birch tree in our backyard and chasing . . . I get ahead of myself. Let me start with right now. You have all your toes and fingers. I counted. The nurse counted. I made the doctor count. The ears are good. The lungs are strong. I heard you cry. This is all good, very good. You are already getting an A. Little fellow. Boy. Son. I do not know what to say. You are my son. You will always be my son. I am your father. I will always be your father. You do not have a name. Your mother will pick the name. When she wakes. There is a list. There are five names on the list. I predict you will get one of the top three. If it were my decision, I would name you Roger. It's a good name. Roger. Roger. No one names their kid Roger. It is not even on the list. Your mother will decide. She knows best. For now, I will call you Roger. Roger, son, let me tell you about your mother. She is beautiful. In every way. You will see. When I first fell in love with your mother, she rejected me. I had lessons to learn and so did she—that is how she sums it up. It seemed our paths would never converge. But some years later—agonizing years— we got a second chance. I cannot explain. Roger, be brave. That's all I can say. Lessons. Math will be easy for you. And fun. Will it? It should be. English too. Do not be a selfish boor. I used to be a hotshot. Do not be a hotshot. I guess it's okay, if you are, but you're never as hot as you think you are. Do not change your name. Do not change it to Roger even though we both know it is a great name. Do whatever your mother tells you to do. It will be my responsibility to say no. "No, Roger, I said no." Once in a while I will say yes. For a whole day . . . on your birthday . . . every October the fifth, I will say yes all day long.

A COMMON MARTYR

Michael Weems

Dramatic
SYDNEY, 20 to 25

SIDNEY *is on a camping trip with friends. He's hunted down by his girlfriend,* KIM, *and unleashes upon her a pent-up diatribe that's been years in waiting.*

SIDNEY   Talk . . . or lecture? Nag. Pester. "Stop looking at birds and start looking at me, Sid." "Not until I see a ring, Sid." "You can't get a job *there*, I'm staying near my folks, Sid." When do I get to talk? Hmm? I know *exactly* what you had in mind. Four years in college together. We lived in adjoining dorms. I checked in on you every night before bed and got that oh-so-incredible peck on the lips to carry me through to my next bland day. Talked about getting engaged in our junior year—a nice-sized rock that's just like the ones you see in magazines, though nothing that's financially attainable by someone—I don't know—like me. And today we graduated together. The next step is getting married next summer in a lavish gala that your family can't afford. You won't be quite ready for sex, as it truly should be foremost about procreation over enjoyment and you want it to be special. As opposed to following my real passion, I'll go off to law school or some graduate program of which I'll have no interest in whatsoever. After I've gotten my worthless master's degree, I'll land in some boring-ass job where I debate on a daily basis whether to push pencils for another day against jumping head first from the twentieth floor and seeing which one hurts more in the long run. By age thirty and either through my having begged for fifteen years or the grace of God, we'll have sex for the first and last time and you'll pump out a child, never working another day of your life. And if we have a boy, odds are you'll start the whole cycle of breaking him down systematically from day one until he's a flaccid, pulp-like cardboard cutout that his father embodies! No thanks. Not for me.

COMPLETENESS
Itamar Moses

Seriocomic
ELLIOTT, 20s

ELLIOTT, *a grad student in computer science, is talking to* MOLLY,
*a molecular biology student, regarding his feelings about their
relationship and with whom he may be in love.*

ELLIOTT   You know, I've been . . . coming to this computer room
a lot, lately, just at random, different times of day, just . . .
Even though it's not remotely convenient for me . . . or on
my way anywhere, but just because I've been I guess . . .
hoping . . . And I know that I probably could have written
to you, or . . . called, I guess, but for some reason I felt like I
was supposed to just . . . [*Beat.*] Molly, I really like you? No,
like, really a lot, and I'm attracted to you, and you're really
smart, and we're interested in a lot of the same things,
and I look forward to seeing you, and I think about you
when you're not around, and so if I seem spare, remote,
well, then, I'm sorry that I seem that way, but I promise
it has nothing to do with not wanting to be close to you,
or . . . wanting to be with other people, or, okay, I mean,
it does, of course it does, a little, I mean, sure, I want to
sleep with every attractive woman I meet, or pass on the
street, or am told about second hand, I mean, you people
don't know what it's like, you think you do, and maybe you
kind of do, in your way, but you don't, not really, you do
not . . . Not that I actually want to go out and sleep with
lots of people, that's an awful lot of work, and it usually
turns out to be more trouble than it's worth, and, I'm getting off topic? What it is is the fear that actually knowing
everything about each other will eliminate the wanting.

And so maybe what I was hoping for was that, this time, if I could hold something just close enough to keep it from disappearing, but just far enough to maintain how I felt about it—which was good, by the way, this felt really really good—then maybe I could draw the first part out a little, because, I don't care about you? But I don't have any compelling evidence that something better will come after this? Even exists. That it ever gets any better than still wanting to be with you, still knowing that I can, or . . . could, because this obviously doesn't work either, does it, so . . . Maybe what's req . . . [*Beat.*] I'm so tired. Of going back and forth. Between failing at this and wondering why I failed. [*Beat.*] I want us to know everything about each other. I want us to know so much about each other that it turns out we know less and less every day. [*Beat.*] Sorry. Too much? Too soon?

CRASHING THE PARTY

Josh Tobiessen

Seriocomic
DAVID JR., 22

DAVID JR. *is fresh out of college. He tells his parents what he wants to do with his life. He wants to do something so meaningful that it will get him on* Charlie Rose.

DAVID JR.   I don't want a job just for the sake of having a job. I want to make a difference somewhere in the world. I want my life to have meaning. Like, I was watching that show *Charlie Rose*, and this guy was on it who had built some schools or something in India? No. Someplace more topical. Afghanistan or something. There were all these pictures of him with these school kids in burkas—or, not the whole burka, but, you know, they looked Middle Eastern. Whatever, the point is that I want to be on *Charlie Rose*. I want to live the kind of life that people want to interview you about. You know, it's like, you're at a cocktail party somewhere wearing some traditional piece of clothing from whatever country you're helping and you're talking to some douchebag in a suit and he's like, "Yeah, I just made blankity-blank amount of money with a hedge fund, what do you do?" And you're like, "I just built a hospital in Bangladesh, dickhead." Bam! You win. And the guy realizes that that he's been wasting his life. I don't know, maybe he suddenly wants to give all his money to your hospital. That's how you make connections. Networking. I mean, at the end of your life you're going to ask yourself, "Did I make a difference? Did I make some children smile?" Answer: Yes. I did. I built a school somewhere. Not here, but in a place where kids actually *like* going to school. I was on *Charlie Rose*. Then you can die happy. Make people cry. All those foreign kids who actually *like* going to school bawling their eyes out. Because now that I'm dead, who's going to help them? No one. They're screwed.

CROSSING THE LINE

J. Thalia Cunningham

Dramatic
EUGENE, early 20s

EUGENE FREER, a young Midwestern U.S. Navy veteran, has just completed his military service and returns home to his wife, EMILY. EUGENE's aberrant behavior is disturbing to EMILY and his best friend, LEO, particularly when EUGENE spends an increasing amount of time in the bathroom with a metal lunchbox he keeps locked and by his side at all times. This searing exploration of male military sexual trauma reveals a facet of military life rarely unveiled to the public. Note: After his suicide attempt with a broken Shasta Root Beer bottle, EUGENE is hospitalized in the psychiatric ward of a VA hospital. Following his assault on another patient, EUGENE finally unburdens himself to his psychiatrist and explains the ritual of Crossing the Line.

EUGENE   They do it in the Navy when the ship crosses the line . . . the equator. It's some tradition . . . supposed to make men out of us . . . loyal to each other. . . . Fella told me it goes back hundreds of years . . . sailors do it all over the world. See, guys who already crossed the equator, they're Shellbacks, sons of King Neptune. Us guys who never crossed the equator, we were slimy Pollywogs. . . . One guy dressed up like King Neptune, beard and all . . . he held that pitchfork thing. . . . Then Davy Jones . . . not that short English guy who sang with the Monkees . . . another Davy Jones . . . something to do with the ocean, okay? During training, some guys started talking about it . . . said some Wogs—that's short for Pollywogs—got beat up so bad, they landed in the hospital . . . some drowned . . . became shark shit.

[*Begins crying.*]

I didn't sign up to die. All I wanted to do was keep up my mortgage payments. What does this have to do with proudly serving America? I got real nervous, but how you gonna back out once you're aboard, huh? Jump off? You're shark shit either way.

[*He is starting to become agitated.*]

Give me a minute. Lemme just get myself together here. Some older fellas said everything got changed back maybe 1991 when some secretary of the Navy issued new instructions about that stuff. There was this meeting in Las Vegas where lots of girls got assaulted—you know—sexually, I mean—by Navy guys—officers—not enlisted men, okay? So I guess this secretary guy said these rituals were okay to make good leaders out of us, help us respect each other. But the Navy wasn't supposed to do anything to embarrass or hurt anyone. Until it started and I realized whatever stupid-ass instruction he issued was all a crock of horseshit. You think some big-deal secretary knows what happens on a ship in the middle of the ocean? Or cares? Shit-fucking-no. He's in his fancy office inside some marble building in Washington that never leaks when it rains. While some asshole politician was signing more instructions and proclamations to get himself on the news, the Shellbacks were forcing us to dress up in women's clothes for a Beauty Bitch Contest. I could stand shaving cream and sticking my face into a toilet and eating garbage off the stomach of Neptune's baby, if that's all they were going to do. How the fuck do eggs squished into your hair and licking disgusting things off somebody's dirty feet make you a better sailor, huh?

CROSSING THE LINE
J. Thalia Cunningham

Dramatic
EUGENE, early 20s

EUGENE FREER, *a young Midwestern U.S. Navy veteran, has just completed his military service and returns home to his wife,* EMILY. EUGENE*'s aberrant behavior is disturbing to* EMILY *and his best friend,* LEO, *particularly when* EUGENE *spends an increasing amount of time in the bathroom with a metal lunchbox he keeps locked and by his side at all times. This searing exploration of male military sexual trauma reveals a facet of military life rarely unveiled to the public. At one point during the play,* EUGENE *is hospitalized in the psychiatric ward of a VA hospital, where he attacks a patient who makes homosexual advances.* EUGENE *finally explains to his psychiatrist what happened on his ship during the Crossing the Line ritual.*

EUGENE   They locked us in coffins of salt water. Felt like I couldn't breathe. I never did learn to swim that good in the few weeks they gave me to learn. They made us strip naked and do the elephant walk. That meant we had to parade around in a line grabbing onto the private parts of the Wog in front of us, while the Wog behind was doing the same thing to me, like elephants walk trunk-to-tail. Everyone was watching and laughing at us, hundreds of people. Girls, too. Then they told us to drop to our hands and knees for the butt bite. So we crawled around on deck, in a long line. I had to put my nose in the asshole of the guy in front of me, biting on his butt, while the Wog behind did it to me. You gotta bite and get bitten hard enough to draw blood. After that, they tested our ability to stand pain. They beat us. With red rubber hoses. Hard, too. Some Shellbacks poured something on Wogs' butts first so it would burn our skin when we got hit. The Shellbacks really got out of control. They started shoving mop handles up inside us, back and forth, in and out, over and over, over and over, over and over. Four or five guys held me down so I couldn't get away. I asked them to stop it stop it stop it, but they just laughed and did it more more more more. It hurt, it hurt more than getting beat with the hose, even with that burning stuff poured on my skin. I begged them, "Please no more, no more no more no more no more no more," but the more I yelled, the more they laughed and kept going. Some officers did it to us, too. There was no one to help me, no one, no one. I hollered for them to stop it stop it stop it stop it stop it stop it, no more no more no more no more no more, but they wouldn't listen to me. I started to cry; couldn't help it. They called me a pussy. A Wog who couldn't take it like a man. Then I felt the first guy shoving his dick into my ass while the other guys held me down. It hurt worse than the mop handle. When he was done, another guy took his place, then another. I tried to get away, but they held me down. I looked around, saw the same thing happening to other guys. I threw up and then, I think I passed out, face-down right in the pile of puke. Next day, my face was crusty with dry chunks of puked-up garbage glued to it. I was so sore, I could hardly walk.

THE DUNES
Craig Pospisil

Dramatic
TROY, 20

TROY, *a local, is* ANNE*'s boyfriend and plays in a local rock band.*
TROY *and* ANNE *overhear a fight between* LAURA, ANNE*'s mother,*
and other family members. When LAURA *discovers* ANNE *and*
TROY *hiding, she treats them rudely before stalking out of the*
room. ANNE *is deeply embarrassed, but* TROY *shrugs it off.*

TROY   Hey, it doesn't matter. I mean . . . nothing matters. The
world's totally fucked. The ocean's full of garbage, but we
still eat the fish, right? Last summer my friend, Mitchell,
he's at this party with his girlfriend and suddenly she says
she wants to break up. Well, Mitchell freaks, can't believe
it. He's super upset. Does a shitload of drugs, gets totally
ripped, and on the way home he flies through a Stop sign
and nails this other car. Mitchell's dead. The couple in the
other car is dead. It was the front-page story in the *Star*.
Pictures of the cars all wrecked and twisted. It was serious.
But after the funeral I'm talkin' to his girlfriend, and she's a
mess. And she tells me, she didn't want to break up, but he
wasn't paying enough attention to her, so she wanted to
get a rise out of him.

[*Slight pause.*]

People suck. That's the way it is. One day your girlfriend
says, "I'm sorry if this ruins your life or anything, but I wanna
to fuck this other guy now. See ya." And a couple months
later that guy's gonna decide he wants to hook up with
some other girl, and so on.

[*Slight pause.*]

Your mom's been screwed by this guy, so she's got to take it out on someone. Me, I'm nobody, so she's a bitch to me. It's no big deal. I'll live. Hey, in some places people shoot each other over who can pray louder. So don't worry about this here.

EMOTION MEMORY

Don Nigro

Seriocomic
STANISLAVSKY, 35

KONSTANTIN STANISLAVSKY *and the Moscow Art Theatre have done a very successful production of Chekhov's* The Seagull, *and they have just given a performance in Yalta for* CHEKHOV, *who was unable to be at the opening.* CHEKHOV, *however, is horrified by what they've done, convinced that they've totally misunderstood his play and just done it badly in a different way from the disastrous earlier production.* STANISLAVSKY *has just asked* CHEKHOV *why, if it was so bad, did the audience clap until their hands bled, and* CHEKHOV *admits that he doesn't know, that it makes no sense to him.* STANISLAVSKY, *a tall, impressive-looking character actor, is desperate to convince* CHEKHOV *not to shut the production down.*

STANISLAVSKY   But that's the thing. It makes no sense. The theater never makes any sense. One night you're a genius, and the next night you're a fool. You think you've played well and they hate it. You think you've played badly and they love it. You do a great play and they despise it. You do a terrible play and they adore it. You're brilliant one night, you think you're doing it exactly the same way the next night, and suddenly they hate you again. You can work ten years on a part and still not understand it. You can understand it with your head and your body won't cooperate. You can know how to move and not have a clue how to speak. You open your mouth and the wrong words come out. You think the audience is hopelessly stupid, and then suddenly they see things you didn't. You think they're smarter than you thought, and then they miss something so obvious a cow would understand it. You work like a dog, and then the sofa catches fire or somebody in the first row vomits on your shoes. They pay people to write horrible things about you in the papers, people who in their whole life have never created anything but turds. It's absolutely maddening. You never get to the bottom of it. I could spend the rest of my life doing *Uncle Vanya* and still there'd be more to it that I hadn't discovered and also that you haven't discovered. It is utterly trivial work. And it is the most important thing I could possibly be doing. It's somehow the key to the entire mad universe. It's investigating the inside of God's brain. It's everything. And if somehow, once in a while, one manages to do good work, despite everything, that is a very precious gift from out of the lunatic toy chest of time and chance, and you mustn't take this away from us. You can't. All right. It's true I didn't appreciate your play at first. Maybe I don't understand it yet. Maybe I just did a wonderful production of a play I don't understand at all. But something happened out there. We might not have found all the truth in it, but we found some of it. And the audience knew it. Each time we perform it we'll find some more. Because your plays are like that. At first, they don't look like much. But once you get inside them, they prey upon your mind, and you can't get rid of them. They have rooms in them that keep opening up into other rooms. It's the most extraordinary thing. I don't know how you do it, and probably you don't know, either. But I do know that I want to spend the rest of my life living inside your plays. Nobody else in the history of the world will ever do your work with the love and attention and obsession that I will devote to them. If there are things I can't see now, I'll find them later. My mistakes will be more interesting than other people's triumphs. I'll get on my knees and beg you if I have to. Don't take this away from me.

EMOTION MEMORY
Don Nigro

Dramatic
CHEKHOV, mid-30s

ANTON CHEKHOV *has been out walking in the cold all night after
the disastrous first performance of his play* The Seagull *at the
Maly Theatre. His friend* LYKA, *who's in love with him and who
has been the model for the character of Nina in the play, has been
waiting up for him all night, very worried. She's just asked him if he
doesn't think the performance went well.*

CHEKHOV   It was a monstrous obscenity. The theater is a
monstrous obscenity. It's an obscene, criminal activity. I
tried to tell them to play it naturally, like life. I told them
again and again. But the simple-minded jackasses just
smiled and nodded their empty heads and ignored me.
Poor fool, they said to each other. He's just a playwright. He
knows nothing about the theater. Arrogant cretins. Even
in my worst nightmares I could not have imagined what
a grotesque abortion they made of my play. People in the
audience were jabbering at each other during the performance, turning their backs to the stage, jeering so loud
you couldn't hear the actors, and maybe it's just as well,
because the actors were totally incompetent. The audience
was moronic, and the critics are cannibalistic orangutans.
I am lectured to about how to write by lip-diddling slugs
who can barely scrawl their own names. The whole thing
was like a scene from hell, with monkeys jumping up and
down, hurling handfuls of excrement. This is what it is to be
a playwright—to be urinated on by satanic monkeys. If I am
ever stupid enough to write another play again, please do
me the kindness of getting a gun and shooting me in the

head. When I was walking, what kept coming into my head was the night my brother died. I sat in the rain, waiting for seven hours for a train to come, in absolute despair, listening to some actors rehearsing some foolish melodrama on the other side of a wall. And it seemed to me that all of my life was plays within plays. Everybody is listening on the other side of a wall to some melodrama which is actually somebody else's life. The plays are all interconnected. The minor characters in the play of your life are major characters in their own plays. And one by one the plays come to an end and the actors leave the stage and then somebody else's play runs for a while, and it goes on until the sun explodes, and then what did it all mean? But while the play was being rehearsed, at least, there was something to give one's attention to. There was some value in that. But I was wrong. There is nothing in the world that can justify sitting in a theater and watching everything that's most precious to you shat upon by malicious cretins. Never again. Never, never again.

THE FALLEN
Yasmine Beverly Rana

Dramatic
ANDREJ, early 20s

It is 1992, and ANDREJ, *a 19-year-old White Eagle Militia member, is in a former school building in Kalinovik, Bosnia, that is used for the detention and systematic rape of Bosnian Muslim women for the purpose of ethnic cleansing. He speaks to Kalinovik prisoner* MIRELA, *a 19-year-old Bosnian Muslim woman.*

ANDREJ   Do you want to kill me? I bet you do. I bet if I turned around and unchained you and if you grabbed my gun, you'd shoot me, not once, but several times, over and over again, until you were sure I was dead. Right? So that's why I'm not . . . letting you go. Not to punish you, but protect myself. This is not about you, but I have to watch out for myself. You could kill me. You want to, right? Say something. Say something so I know you're alive. I have to keep you alive for the next guy. [*Laughs.*] Or else I get in trouble, and I don't want to get into trouble. I don't need any trouble. [*Beat.*] Aren't you sick of this? I am. I don't even think you're pretty or anything like that. You're not my type. You're not ugly, you're just . . . someone I'd never notice. [*Beat.*] No, I would notice. I would, because you're nice. I think you are . . . I really don't know you. You won't talk to me, but I can guess, yeah? I know you hate me. I hate myself, kind of. But this is not really my fault, you know. I didn't start this! Look at yourself for that! Yeah . . . well, I don't know anything. I just . . . I just go along with it all, you know? [*Beat.*] No, wait, you . . . you're okay looking. Pretty, a little. Say something. I don't want to hurt you, but I need you to speak. I don't even know what your voice sounds like.

Maybe you lost it. Maybe you can't speak anymore. Then that's okay. Then I know . . . it's not because of me, just me. I won't be hurt. [*Quietly distraught.*] I never hurt anyone before this. I never did. I would never have done anything . . . like this! Like this? Whatever this is . . . I still don't understand it, but I was never good enough at school to understand anything. So I never asked about anything. It's not like I didn't care . . . it was more like . . . why should I care? Did you care? I think you did. You're looking into the distance and I don't even know what you're looking at. What is it? A hole in the wall? A fly? Air? Whatever air looks like. What does it like? I don't know. [*Chuckles.*] I don't even want kids. I don't even know you. Why would I want a kid with you? This makes no sense. I don't get it. I wish you could explain this to me, because I'm lost, right now. [*Beat.*] But I always was. I don't know where I am. But you know where we are. You're very aware of where we are and what this is.

FETCH CLAY, MAKE MAN
Will Power

Comic
MUHAMMAD ALI, mid-20s

MUHAMMAD ALI, *who has just changed his name from* CASSIUS CLAY, *is about to fight* SONNY LISTON *for the second time. He has brought into his entourage the old-time movie comedian* LINCOLN PERRY, *better known as Stepin Fetchit, who has suggested that* JOHN FORD *would be the perfect director for a movie about* ALI's *life.*

MUHAMMAD ALI   Well, I like a Western as much as the next guy, but I just can't see it for my story—no we got to get a brother in the Nation to do it. If you sayin' you concerned about how the White Man bends the way I look and what I say on television, well what's to say John Ford wouldn't do the same thing? He ain't one a us, and no tellin' what he might do . . . damn he might have me gettin' beat up by some old cowboy or something. Now what would my fans say if they go to the movies and see me, the greatest of all times, gettin' beat up by some cowboy? I mean I wouldn't mind if I lost to the Mummy or something like that, 'cause they got supernatural powers. Plus the Mummy is from Egypt, and Egypt is in Africa, which means the Mummy is a brother, you dig? And if I gotta get knocked out, I'd rather lose to a supernatural brother than a raggedy old cowboy. Man I could see it now, the new Black Man vs. the old Black Man. And then at the end, right as we about to get it on, we realize that despite our differences, we one in the same. Only thing is he wrapped up in all them bandages and you can still see me pretty, but besides that we both the same—two black men—and me and the Mummy join in the struggle together. Now that would be a movie.

FIVE MILE LAKE
Rachel Bonds

Seriocomic
RUFUS, mid- to late 20s

RUFUS *tells his friend* JASON *about* PETA, *his new girlfriend, who coldcocked a guy in a bar the night* RUFUS *met her.*

RUFUS   So then *he*—he then tries to *recover* and pretends that he DIDN'T say what he just said, like tries to coast over it *entirely*—and she's standing there with like, mouth agape, like—"What the fuuuuuuck did you just say?"—and he's like fumbling around saying like, "Well anyway, what I meant was, see what I'm trying to say is blah blah" and while he's like shitting his pants she just like . . . ohmygod— she just *rears back* and—

[*He gestures a sucker punch.*]

WHAM! She just rears back and punches the guy right in the face. And then like the whole room goes quiet and he's clutching his face and making this *weird* whimpering sound and everyone's staring at him, except for me—because I'm looking at *her*—and you can barely see it, like it's barely there, it's just this tiny, tiny, tiny thing, but I see it. She has this subtle, little snarl going on. Like her lip is slightly curved up on one side—it's really small, like almost imperceptible—but it's there—this like real *animal* thing. And that's it, then I'm just like, "I must know this girl. This girl must be in my daily life from now on." Just . . . I mean she really beat the shit out of him. And then that little *snarl*. How do you not walk across the room and immediately introduce yourself to that girl?

FOURTEEN HUNDRED AND SIXTY SKECTHES OF YOUR LEFT HAND

Duncan Pflaster

Dramatic
ALONSO: 20, Latino

ALONSO *is a young painter with temporal lobe epilepsy. He is speaking to his art school friend* PAUL, *on whom he's had a huge crush.* PAUL *has come to stay for the summer with* ALONSO *and his sister* BLANCA, *who has enlisted* PAUL *to keep* ALONSO *taking his medication.*

ALONSO   Look, taking the pills dampens everything down for me. It's like wearing a blindfold made of a black-and-white movie. I can't do it. There's that Leonard Cohen line: "There is a crack in everything. That's how the light gets in." The broken part is where the art comes from. I can't paint, I can't do it, I can't do anything right when I'm on these fucking pills. People didn't have these pills in olden times. Like they didn't have dentists. And they were fine. All my life I've been told I had a special gift. That my art was something magical. I liked it, I wanted to be special. A brilliant, tortured artist. Right? We all fall for that image. But then I went to college and met you and a bunch of other tortured artists, and we were all special. I mean, you remember Lenny, with his fauvist style? All those bright colors just exploding everywhere. And Sarah's intricate line work, so tight and controlled. How could I compete with Monti, who made me cry once with a painting of Dominick's elbow? And god: and you. We were all the gifted children wherever we came from, and I had no idea how to cope once I got in with everyone who was just as talented and special and stressed just like me. I had to up my game. And then I realized that this talent, this weirdness I have of seeing things a different way, that's what really makes me special. I don't see things like anyone else, so I don't paint like anyone else. I am unique. Without my fucked-up brain, what am I? We're shooting stars, that's all we are. Burn brightly, then fade away. Wouldn't you give your life up if it meant that you could be the genius you always knew you were? And you are a genius, my friend; don't be bashful, you know that. If someone was going to take that away, but let you live forever, would you take that bargain?

FOURTEEN HUNDRED AND SIXTY SKETCHES OF YOUR LEFT HAND

Duncan Pflaster

Seriocomic
GABRIEL, 32

GABRIEL *is a soldier who's come to propose to his girlfriend*
BLANCA *while on leave from the army. Unbeknownst to him, she's*
been having an affair with a painter named PAUL, *who's staying*
with her brother ALONSO *and her for the summer. When* GABRIEL
arrives, PAUL *manipulates him into posing nude for him and*
ALONSO. GABRIEL *speaks to the audience as he delivers his inner*
monologue during the painting session.

GABRIEL   Yeah, I know I've got a good body. I work out. And
God blessed me with a pretty good dick. It does what I
need it to, when I want it to. Girls are usually impressed.
And I've never had any complaints. And you know, part of
having a nice body, part of working to have a nice body,
is that you want people to look. You want people to check
out the merchandise and approve. But this shit is different.
I mean, not because Alonso and Paul are dudes—other
dudes check me out all the time, and it's like whatever, jealous guys who want to be me, or homos checking me out
in the gym who wish they could get up on this, you know. I
let 'em look. I'm a man. Or, you know, showering with other
dudes in the army, you sometimes have to see other guys
briefly out of the corner of your eye, just when they end
up in your periphery. Or pranks. There's nothing funnier
than getting some poor bastard friend of yours stripped
and humiliated. I mean, we're way beyond just Sharpieing
a dick on a bro's face. That's amateur. We make an art out
of it. We totally got Danny a few days before I left, got him

completely wasted: he woke up naked, painted blue except for his little dick and with an American flag stuck in his ass. And last month poor Scotty passed out drunk and got tea-bagged by the entire barracks; there's video up on YouTube, it's a private link, but we've all seen it. Even I've got pranked a couple of times. Once I woke up bare-ass 12-50 naked, Saran-wrapped to my buddy Adam. Who was also naked. And they cracked some eggs on us. And Adam got Scott's dick rubbed on his face as revenge for the tea-bagging. There were so many pictures of that shit. It's just guys having fun, and when it's all guys, you get to know what you all look like naked. It's a status thing. If you can get your buddy to acknowledge that you're superior, you win. It's just part of being a man, right? So I am totally cool with being seen without clothes on. But this is different. Actually sitting. Voluntarily. Inviting them to look. Naw, they're not just looking, they're studying me. I've never had anyone just stare at my body for this long. This is kind of uncomfortable. You done drawing my dick yet?

GEORGIE GETS A FACELIFT
Daniel Guyton

Dramatic
GEORGIE, 20s

GEORGIE *is a troubled man. He has just killed a Girl Scout by accident, to whose body he addresses this monologue.*

GEORGIE   Let me tell you a *lesson* about *life*! Okay? Life is not . . . What do you do? You sell Girl Scout cookies? Okay, let me tell you something. What do you gotta sell? Like three hundred of them? Okay. Let's just say you gotta sell, like, three hundred Thin Mints, okay? Like you got, okay, you got, like, three hundred *boxes* of Thin Mints, right? Okay, you got three hundred boxes of Thin Mints because those are the *cookies* that everybody loves, right? Okay, so here you are, you're sellin' 'em. "Whoop de doo! Buy my Thin Mints!" Right? So, what happens? You sell three hundred Thin Mints and what do you get? A medal? A fuckin' *patch* on your shawl that says "Look at *me*, I sold three hundred *boxes* of THIN MINTS?!?" Is that what it's *for*? A fucking PATCH?!?

[*He calms down.*]

Well, that's cool. Because I mean, you know, patches are nice. They add a little color, a little . . . flavor to your brown and green. But . . . you just don't *understand*. You just don't under*stand* that for every *patch* you receive in life, there will be some motherfucker ready to stab you in the back and steal your patch *away* from you!!! You just don't understand this.

[*He cries.*]

And I'm teaching you a lesson. There will be some *mother* . . . You just don't understand. You're just a little girl. [*Pause.*] I had a patch, too, once. You think I'm a monster, but I had a patch, *too*. It was called a bachelor's degree. I thought, "I could own the world." Spent six years in college and I thought, "Man, I finally got it right." Spent six years in . . . I finally got it right. I thought, "Now I can get a job. Now I can do something with my life." You think I'm a monster. You think I'm a monster 'cause I shot you, don't you? You think . . . Well, I'm not a monster. I only did it 'cause I care. I only did it 'cause . . .

[*He stands.*]

You're right, I *am* a monster. They took my *job* away! What else could I do? I spent six years in *college* and they took my *job* away! I . . . What else could I *do*? They stabbed me in the back and took my job away. Just one mistake and they never let it die. Just . . . one mistake. And they *never* let it die. I just want my patch.

GOLDEN AGE
Terrence McNally

Seriocomic
FLORIMO, late 20s to early 30s

We are at the opening night of VINCENZO BELLINI*'s* I Puritani. *FLORIMO,* BELLINI*'s lover, is talking to him about the day*
BELLINI *composed the opera. The Malibran is a famous, tem-
peramental soprano.*

FLORIMO   I remember the morning you composed it. We
   were in a villa overlooking Lake Como that one of your
   admirers had lent you. There were birds sweeping back and
   forth, back and forth over the lake, waiting to dive down
   and snatch up some unsuspecting fish in an act of neces-
   sity that seemed like random violence to someone lying in
   bed watching them through open French doors and you at
   an ill-tuned piano in a terrible mood composing this very
   music while hung-over from the night before. We'd drunk
   only champagne. Someone had told us that if we drank
   only champagne we wouldn't have a hang-over but if we
   mixed the champagne with even a sip of anything else, all
   bets were off. It was the Malibran. She would know. She is
   the mistress of debauchery. I made sure I drank only champagne that evening—you, too, my love—and we drank it
   copiously. I was delighted to prove her right. We got won-
   drously loaded. We sang, we danced, we broke furniture,
   we peed off the balcony and jeered at the moon. We toast-
   ed the Malibran again and again for the gift of intoxication
   without remorse. What a tumultuous, fucked-up drunken
   night. Suddenly somehow it was the next morning. I don't
   think I've ever woken up with a worse headache. When
   I challenged the Malibran, she said obviously we hadn't

been drinking French champagne. All other champagnes gave you a hang-over. Only French champagne didn't. I told her she was full of shit and, if not shit, of herself—and maybe they were the same thing. She said, "Of course I am but you're the only person who would dare to tell me so." I don't think your friends and colleagues know what to make of me. I'm not an artist. I don't create. I can't do what you do. They think I keep your bed warm when no one else is in it. That's not even the half of it. I remember lying there that morning, looking at you across the room, barefoot in your nightshirt, hair crazy and uncombed, bent over the keyboard, hollow-eyed, beautiful, beautiful to me, oblivious to me, me watching you do what you do and falling in love with you all over again. I got aroused. I wanted to call you back to bed but I knew better. Besides, you wouldn't have heard me. And then suddenly you were finished and you looked over at me still lying in bed and you said, "It's done. I think it might be all right. May I play it for you?" You were like a little boy and you began to play this same music and sing in your own, almost truly awful voice. No one sings Bellini like you, certainly they don't—even if they are the four greatest voices in the world. The world has the Puritans Quartet, I had Bellini himself. I was present at the creation. I was your world premiere. The Malibrans, the Grisis, the Rubinis can't take that away from me. I heard it first. It was beautiful. We both knew it.

GOLDEN AGE
Terrence McNally

Seriocomic
BELLINI, 33

VINCENZO BELLINI, *the composer of the opera* I Puritani, *is backstage during the opening night performance, talking to some singers while they wait to go back on.*

BELLINI   "Write us a comedy." They don't take me seriously. They take my music very seriously but not me. "Write us a comedy." I want to write *The Puritans*. Yes, it's a ridiculous libretto but my music isn't. "Write us a comedy." Never "How can we serve you? What do you want to write, maestro?" The next time it will be the opera I want to write. There will be no literal-minded poet to drag me down with a pedestrian libretto. There will be no egos to satisfy but my own, which is so enormous it frightens me. No singers to flatter by composing to their strengths. Rubini wants high notes, Grisi wants mad scenes. I have become their slave and it's driving me mad. I hate mad scenes. People don't go mad because of a broken heart. They take to their rooms and weep in utter solitude. There is no cause for high notes when your heart is broken. The very lowest reaches of the voice are what are called for. I shall write a mad scene for Lablache. A mad scene for a bass! That would be a little more like it. Rossini thinks he wrote one in *Semiramis*, but it was a shallow exercise in note spinning. People thought it was original because no one had done it before. That's a narrow definition of originality. I will give Lablache a mad scene in *Lear* that will terrify him. He will be frightened to sing it. He'll be unable to. The highest art should be unperformable. My masterpiece will be an opera that cannot be performed. What they call art is artifice. No, what I call art is as free, as wild, as unmanageable as life itself. Away with structure. Only feeling matters.

GOOD TELEVISION
Rod MacLachlan

Seriocomic
MACKSON, 23

MACKSON *is talking to* CONNIE, *a TV producer who does a reality show about addiction that involves a family coping with the addiction of one of its members and his rehab.* MACKSON *wants to participate in the show.* CLEMMY *(short for* CLEMSON*) is* MACKSON's *brother and is a crystal meth addict.* BRITTANY *is* MACKSON's *sister.*

MACKSON Hey, you mind if I ask you, I watch your show, its fantastic, really good television. Can I ask you, that drug addict treatment is really expensive, right? So you got that in your budget? You pay for all that rehab, what you got maybe . . . well, some of your shows got two addicts, some just one . . . so lets say eighteen addicts a season times a hundred thousand dollars . . . 'Cause, I was gonna say, that's like almost 2 million dollars . . . Well, its a gift for you . . . for the addict its sort of like selling their life rights, really. Innit? The rehab joint gets their plug, Clemmy gets your super-duper rehab, in return for lettin' you show the whole world he's toothless and all messed up. It's like he sold his life rights to you, but instead of money he gets detox. But for you guys, all that rehab you're offerin' is pure gift. [*Pause.*] Which is fair. I love the show, I love what ya'll do. I was the one that made that audition tape happen, you know. I showed Brit how to use the camera, and I coached 'em. Just on how to do the tape. Just what the tape is supposed to be. [*Beat.*] I wanna say, seriously, I'm ready to do my part. I feel bad about all this. I knew I wasn't really helping enough. Everything fell apart for Clemmy and Brit when Daddy flew the coop. I was twenty-two and wanted to get myself started in my career. Was I . . . was I selfish? Brittany thinks I was. Maybe she's right. So fuck it, I did leave 'em in the lurch and now I intend to use my knowledge to help my family out. And, sure, I would certainly appreciate your help. If you can get him all this expensive rehab and interventions and all this, hey, I'm on the team. Hundred percent.

GOOD TELEVISION
Rod MacLachlan

Dramatic
ETHAN, 33

ETHAN *is the director of a reality TV show about addicts, their rehabilitation, and their families. He is laying into* CONNIE, *the producer. Because of her, an episode got screwed up.*

ETHAN   I knew exactly what to do. I SHOT it. But because things got a little messy, not according to your perfect world recovery script, we lost the episode and a chance to do some good for the MacAddys. I think you of all people should see the problem with that. I know you've had your own struggle with addiction . . . And I know that you lost some addicts in the past, and that's got to be tough . . . and I bet you're honest enough to admit that there's a tendency among addictive personalities to view everything in black-and-white terms. I don't think I need a degree to see you've got some issues you're not willing to face. You all talk about being documentary. Is it really documentary if your recovery rate is 70 percent? Is that showing the truth? Or just making sure everyone feels heroic and nonexploitative? I understand now how painful it is to see an addict fail. So it makes sense you've convinced yourself, and everyone else here, that to be compelling television, every episode needs an up ending. But in fact, showing the truth is compelling television. The *reality* of it . . . no matter what the ending is. So whether Clemmy got a by-the-book intervention or not, I think we could have convinced him to finish our show and offered him treatment at a decent center. BUT, if he still said no, I'd shoot that. Because our show *is* documentary. And there might be failures, not because our schedule is tight, but because our show is about drug addicts. And drunks. And anorexics. We make documentaries about people trying to die. Your choice of subjects—that wasn't about making good television . . . it was about you protecting your comfort level.

GREEN SOUND
John Patrick Bray

Seriocomic
TAYLOR, mid-30s

TAYLOR *has come to* MOLLY*'s apartment holding a lamp that had been hanging in a coffee shop over a table where* TAYLOR *had seen* MOLLY *sit.* MOLLY *stopped going to the coffee shop, which prompted* TAYLOR *to tear the lamp from the ceiling and, screwing up the courage, knock on her door. He is standing there, holding the lamp as* MOLLY *answers. This is their first time meeting.*

TAYLOR   It doesn't look right. This. This here. This light. It doesn't make any sense. Over a table. Without you there. And so, I sat there, in the coffee shop, looking at other people, being touched by the light. And I was . . . sad. I sit there at 11:32 every day. And I leave at 1:01 every day. I take a long lunch. It takes me awhile to eat a muffin. And you arrive between 11:43 and 11:52. You get a coffee. You sit under this light. The same light. I saw you sit there. Four days in a row. Most people don't sit. They leave. But you sit. Somehow at the same table. Under the same light. And when the light shines on other people. Nothing happens. Yes. It doesn't work. It's not right. You haven't been there for three days. And. And. You have a table. May I stand on it? I am not an electrician. I'm a phenomenologist. It's like an electrician. Sort of. I mean. I believe if you peel away structures: words, conversations, the way we're told to be- have, all of it. I believe there is essence underneath. Codes. We're being coded. So, you peel away the codes. Find the essence. But then, if you peel away the essence there are more structures. [*Beat.*] I'm not supposed to steal lights, you know. No one stopped me. I don't know why. I know the manager was looking. He has a beard that he colors. He is losing hair but keeps his hair in a ponytail, pulling more hair off of his head. He has a wart on his nose, and a laugh that is very loud and I think people like to hear his laugh. He wasn't laughing when I took this light. So. [*Beat.*] I think he called the police. But. I didn't see any police so I came right here because I followed you once so I know you lived here. I wanted to say something to you but I couldn't say anything because the words wouldn't make sense and I needed to give you something so this is it. Because, that's the thing with words. If you peel those away, there is more essence. It continues. At the bottom is something outside of discourse. Words, I mean. There is something we can know, I mean. Can't know. Something we can't know. But it doesn't mean it isn't there. And. When you were under the light. I felt like the answer was somehow closer.

HONKY
Greg Kalleres

Dramatic
PETER: 20s, Caucasian

*After weeks of apologizing for being white, PETER finally tells
his therapist, an African American woman, that he's sick of
feeling guilty.*

PETER   What more do I have to do?! Huh!? I *feel* for your people! Okay? The struggle? The, the *plight*?! I have professed
my sins! Every week I come to you, contrite! And out there,
all the time, in different ways! I am sorry! Okay?! I AM SORRY
FOR MY PEOPLE! They *suck*! Whatever they did, whenever
they did it, I renounce them! THEY ARE RENOUNCED! Jesus!
I'm tired of paying for shit I didn't do! Slavery! Oppres-
sion! Forty acres and the Jim Croce laws! I didn't bring you
people over here!

[*Beat.*]

So, I see these black kids on the subway. They look a little
sketchy and I think, "Hey, maybe I should go to the other
side of the train"—but no! Because then I say to myself,
"Who are *you* to judge?! They're probably very smart educated kids! Who am I to assume that just because they're
African American, they don't read Sartre?!" But guess
what?! They pulled a *fucking gun* on me anyway! It didn't
matter what I thought! So fuck them! And fuck *guilt*!! I'm
tired of it!! Watching my tongue, policing every syllable
that comes out of my mouth! So, do me a favor, will you?
Tell every black person or African American that you know
that it wasn't me! Can you do that? Vouch for me?! Huh? IT!
WASN'T! ME!

[*Beat.*]

Whoa. That felt really good. Was that a *breakthrough?* Is that what they call it or whatever? I'm sorry if I scared you—did I? Jesus, that was amazing! Well . . . I guess I should probably go. Thank you.

HOW TO GET INTO BUILDINGS
Trish Harnetiaux

Comic
ETHAN, 30s

ETHAN *is talking to* DAPHNE, *trying to woo her, to impress her with his ability to understand himself and his past and how it has made him the man he is today. He is earnest, passionate, and self-assured. This is a flirtatious yet confessional moment for him.*

ETHAN   If you really want to know, fine . . . I'll tell you; it's a simple story, amusing. Okay, here we go: I wanted to be a doctor, but my mother wanted me to be a waiter. I want to learn about the heart, she wants me to serve artichoke hearts with a garlic aioli dipping sauce. I eventually caved and found the best restaurant in town: I walked in and am like, "I want to be a waiter. *Here.*" And he's like, "You have no experience." And I looked him in the eye and am like, "Okay man, I'll be a busser." And he's like, "No." And I'm like, "I will be a dishwasher." And he's like, "No." And I'm like, "Okay—I'll be a FREE dishwasher." And he's like . . . "No." I don't tell that to many people . . . It never would have happened without your encouragement, Daphne. Your persistence. Your enthusiasm. Your cool hair. I was at a convention. Before the book, in real life, after I left Zenn-La. There was a presentation by: A Man. He spoke for hours and hours on the subject of life, of love, of How To Get Into Buildings. There was fire, images, music. There was something strangely intriguing about him. There actually was a fire, so I never heard the end of his speech but I *trusted* him. There was a sadness behind his eyes and a fierceness to his cadence, he inspired and endeared. He spoke about the uniform of a Pizza Delivery Guy. About its potential. He spoke, and I listened.

HOW TO GET INTO BUILDINGS
Trish Harnetiaux

Comic
ROGER, 20s

This is ROGER's *Big Moment. He is finally giving his presentation at Comic Con this year—it's his guide to survival for the modern man or woman. He believes deeply in his well-developed philosophies and has been waiting for this moment, the platform where he will share his ideas with the world.*

ROGER   Good afternoon Ladies and Gentlemen, Superheroes, and Lords of the Underworld . . . What people today, in our society, on Earth, don't realize, is that most buildings are just that: *buildings.* They are buildings with *people* in them. You, or one, may, for instance, just walk in the door. Just go into a building and say, "Hey, is the superintendent around?" And they're like, "What?" And you say, more forcefully, "Hey—is the super here." And sometimes they say, "No, come back after lunch." And you should just say, "Cool," or something, and just hang out for a bit, outside or at Starbucks, and then go back after lunch and start it all again. *Persistence.* You may think you know what you want to "study" or "be," but I'm telling you right now, don't go running around like a child saying "I'm going to be a Doctor when I grown up." Because you'll be lucky if you're a Waiter. *Lucky. So stop speculating, everyone*! You know? Right now you're all just *speculating. Speculating.* The great thing that I was never told and that I wish I knew at a much younger age is this: The world is just a bunch of people, dude. You have to be ready to BE one of them. And you can be annoying or persistent—that's totally fine! One way modern men, and women, meet people is to dress as a common Pizza

Delivery Guy, or Gal, and enter a building. Tips to ensure entrance include: Make sure you carry the pizza box as if there is a pizza inside. People apparently will let someone with a pizza in ANYWHERE. "I'm here to see Mr. Carmichael on the twenty-first floor." "Go right up." "Nancy from accounting ordered a deep-dish Hawaiian. Which floor is she on again?" "Eleven. Lucky Nancy!" Whether there's a pizza actually IN the box or not, that's up to you. **Because you are just a dude trying to figure out a way into a building.** Into a club. It's one big club, and with persistence, if you stop speculating, and if you show up ready to deliver a pizza, you'll have a fair chance of getting in. So, be sure you show up with a pizza box, and get ready for a waterfall effect or snowball effect of life's big elements to start happening to you. They'll be like:

Grab a chair!

There's your desk!

Here's your cool new cards!

That's your phone!

Meet your wife!

There's your kids!

Board meeting at noon!

Last one to the diner has to buy!

Now look at you. You're in the building, in the club—hell you're on your way to being President of the club. I for one, couldn't be more proud because it's an awful world out there, but look at you, you just made it. You made it.

HOW WATER BEHAVES
Sherry Kramer

Dramatic
STEVE, mid- to late 20s

STEVE *lost his job and he and his wife,* NAN, *are in dire financial straits. In order to participate in the Christmas season, they started a bogus charity and sent all their friends and family notifications saying that they had donated in their friends' and family members' names. Now Christmas is over, and* NAN *wants to go on with their lives and start a family. But* STEVE *says they can't—they owe all the money to charity that they pretended to donate, and they have to actually donate it before they can think about having a baby.*

STEVE   What did you think? That this was a freebie—a fantasy—that there were no consequences? You wanted to pretend to save the world, and feel good about it, and then
go on with your life? Why do you think people don't repair
the world? Because they're cheap? Because they're lazy?
Because they just didn't think of it? You think it's some new
idea you had, and now that you're spreading the word,
everybody is going to say, "Why didn't I think of that? Now
that you've enlightened me, sign me up, I'm on board."
No, Nan. People wake up, every day, and they think, "I can
repair the world, or I can fix my car. I can repair the world,
or send my kid to college." And a couple thousand times,
waking up like that, they stop thinking about repairing the
world at all. Repairing the world is for rich people, not us.
We don't get to do it. They do. It is the ultimate right and
privilege of the rich. I'm not saying it's wrong to want to
change the world, and make it better. Everybody wants a
piece of that. The little people give in dribs and drabs, they
race for the cure, they band together, they raise this or

that. And they give a bigger percentage of their worth to charity than the rich, everywhere on earth. But they could give it all, and it wouldn't matter. Grow up, Nan. There are people in America with more wealth than entire countries. You know how every country changes the course of its rivers, sooner or later? To make damns or to control flooding or just for the fucking sheer hell of it? That's how much money you need to make a difference. You need enough to control the course of the river of money that flows through the world. You need to control that flow. And if you can't do that, then you're just a bobbing cork at the mercy of the current. The reason why people don't repair the world is because they can't afford it. We can't afford it. But we made a pledge to do it anyway. That pledge comes with a cost. A cost you don't want to pay. But I have to, Nan. So you keep living in your fantasy! Keep idolizing Melinda Gates! But guess what? The rich *are* different from you and me. THEY HAVE MONEY.

THE HUNTER'S MOON
Frederick Stroppel

Comic
SHEP, early 30s

SHEP *is a hapless loser type who's hanging out in a neighborhood bar late at night. It's close to Hallowe'en, and when* SHEP *gets scared by his friend* COONEY *wearing a werewolf mask, it prompts him to relate a story to* COONEY *and the bartender,* JIMMY, *about his frightening encounter with what he believes was a real wolf some years earlier.*

SHEP   I had a very bad experience with a wolf. I was up in the Catskills. It was one of those "relive Woodstock" festivals. Except the bands sucked. Anyway, I was in this tent, with this fat chick, and she was snoring like a bull. I couldn't get to sleep, but it was her tent so I couldn't make an issue of it. So it's the middle of the night, and I hear something sniffing around outside, and I try to ignore it, I'm thinking it's just a raccoon or something, but then I hear this water trickling, and I realize it's pissing right on the tent! And I guess she didn't set it up right because it's leaking right through. So I jump out, ready to chase the little bastard off, and right there in front of me is the biggest fucking wolf I ever saw. We're like eye to eye. And it starts showing its teeth. And I'm like, "This is it. I'm dead." Plus I'm totally naked, so he's got, you know, the whole smorgasborg to pick from. Anyway, the fat chick—her name was Patsy, as I recall—she leaps out of the tent with this crossbow—I don't know where the fuck she got that— and she screams, "Yaaagh!" and fires an arrow, totally misses the wolf—I think she hit somebody's car—but the wolf gets spooked and runs off. So I survived. But that was it for me with all the outdoor festivals and being-one-with-nature shit. You know, give me suburbia or give me death.

IF YOU START A FIRE (BE PREPARED TO BURN)

Kevin Kautzman

Seriocomic
CHRIS, 20s

CHRIS, *a college dropout with two years of undergraduate philosophy under his secondhand belt, drives a local truck route. He arrives home to the apartment where his cohabitating waitress-girlfriend* LUCY *is busily preparing a presentation, working toward her* MBA. *She only wants to sell out if they'll just let her. It is revealed* CHRIS *has been fired for punching a coworker, and so, with their backs against a financial wall,* CHRIS *attempts to convince* LUCY *they should start a livecam sex website . . . with her as the star.*

CHRIS   You can quit waiting tables. We'll work from home. Manage our own schedules. We'll take a holiday whenever we want. And nobody will touch you. You'll serve up an idea of yourself, and you'll get your life back in exchange. You will transcend your body. You'll be like an angel. A sex angel! We can get by on my unemployment while we launch a personal, insider website. It's all about the impression of access. And it has to be hot! That's what we'll call it! Hot . . . heat . . . something . . . America? Hot. Heat. America. America in Heat dot-com! It's perfect! Yeah. We take a set of still photos, do a teaser trailer, generate buzz, and sell a subscription for insider content and access to a live webcam and chat room. There are vast networks where people register to access adult content. It is the twenty-first century! People don't live ethically! We can't. We can only live aesthetically! We live in a house of mirrors built on a house of cards built on a foundation of sand! And I'm telling you there is freedom in hopelessness! God or whatever isn't going to descend from heaven and scold you because you show your tits and ass to strangers for money. This machine is powerful. It's a magic box! It can connect us to people with money who want what we have! Youth. And beauty. And purity. Yeah. That's how we'll market you. You're the girl next door. Apple pie. A rainy day at the cabin. You're stranded and without firewood, but someone's at the door with some wood, and he's going to help keep you warm inside your blanket. Which is an American flag! Boom!

Think about it. Nobody cares whether we have any dignity. Insurance. What happens if you get pregnant? We'd have to beg. And I don't want to beg. And I don't want to take out any more loans. They only care if you pay them to care. Socialism lost. Everything's for sale. You can build a cult, a umm . . . a fandom. When people subscribe to your website, you make money. Look at it like this: ten thousand people at ten dollars a year is a hundred thousand dollars. With that kind of money, we could finally afford to stop renting. Buy a house. Start a family. You can golf!

A KID LIKE JAKE
Daniel Pearle

Dramatic
GREG, 30s

GREG and his wife, ALEX, are eager to get their son JAKE into kindergarten at a top private school. JAKE is very bright but lately has started acting out at home and on his school visits, where he's been teased for his gender-nonconforming behavior. GREG is talking to JUDY, the headmistress of JAKE's preschool, who has been advising GREG and ALEX throughout the process.

GREG   We had a bit of a meltdown. Last week. [*Pause.*] Jake wanted to be Snow White for Halloween. And I had said, you know, we could talk about it. But Alex felt strongly it was a bad idea. She's obviously fine with his wearing anything, you know, around the apartment, but she was convinced letting him trick-or-treat like that—in the building . . . That neighbors might look at him funny. And she's right that he's observant. And sensitive. Anyway, we'd kinda been delaying the conversation and Halloween rolls around and Alex has a pirate outfit and a skeleton costume laid out for him on his bed and he asks, what about Snow White? And she tells him she doesn't have a Snow White costume but she has these other costumes, and he says he doesn't like these other costumes. And she tries to explain, you know, sometimes you can't have exactly what you want but that's why we have to compromise. And he starts throwing a tantrum. Says he doesn't want to be a skeleton, that her ideas are *lazy*, "*lazy* ideas"—who knows where he— . . . Eventually she said if he wouldn't stop behaving this way he wouldn't be allowed to go trick-or-treating at all and that really sent him over the edge. Screaming at her. "You *lied* to me . . . You're not my *boss*. Daddy said I could." And I kept explaining I hadn't actually said yes but at that point . . . I mean the two of them were really getting into it. She said he was being a baby, that he didn't deserve a costume at all. And he said . . . you know, "You're the worst mom in the entire world and I wish you were *dead*."

[*He half-laughs, a little embarrassed.*]

Alex thinks maybe we give in too much. He's got all these interviews happening and they're obviously not on his terms and she feels like we owe it to him to set clearer boundaries at home. So he can learn a little more . . . self-control. I don't know. I do worry that he's a little—spoiled. I mean he's an only child, he's got Alex around all the time, a lotta kids don't have that, not to mention, you know, his own *playroom*. It used to be an office—that we shared. I never understood why his toys couldn't just live in his— Anyway, all I'm saying is he is accustomed to getting what he wants. So . . . maybe she has a point.

LAST FIRST KISS
Chad Beckim

Dramatic
PETER, 18

PETER's prom date, GABBY, *has just seen him kissing another boy, and he is trying to explain, and to console her.*

PETER This isn't going to make much sense to you because this doesn't make much sense to me, but I'm going to say it because if I stop to think about it I might not ever say it. Okay? So just let me talk and then we'll deal with the aftermath. [*Takes a breath, begins.*] When I was eight, I caught my mom stuffing my Christmas stocking. Caught her red-handed, hand in the stocking, assorted trinkets in her other hand, no room for explanation. So at eight? No Santa—he's dead to me. So I know this—fact—there is no Santa. But even after that, even after I knew, I wanted so badly to believe in Santa that I, what, I tricked myself. For another three years I tricked myself. And now? We're here. But that's not all . . . you ready? Here goes . . . I love you, Gabby. I really do. When we started . . . dating . . . I kept thinking that things would, whatever, change and all that. That I would become attracted to who I am supposed to be attracted to. That didn't happen. And I'm sorry for that. But it doesn't change the fact that I love you, in spite of me, because of, because . . . you are the best person I know. The best. There's no denying that. You are the best. And I am sorry, Gab. You have no idea how sorry I am that this happened tonight, of all nights. I never would have planned this, you have to understand that, never in a million years, because that would make me slime. It just happened. You have to believe that. BUT . . . if there were ever going to be someone, a girl—no, a woman . . . it would . . . be you. And I don't mean that in some sort of, cereal box, consolation prize way, but in a way that's as honest as anything I can ever say. If there was? It would be you. Does that make sense?

LEGACIES
Kermit Frazier

Dramatic
CARLETON: 27, African American

Speaking to his 16-year-old nephew, JOSEPH, near a bench in the park, CARLETON tells the story of his recently traveling to Washington, DC, to view his older brother's name on the Vietnam Memorial.

CARLETON   I took me a bus trip to DC last weekend. Went there to see the Vietnam thing. The memorial. Went by myself. Didn't tell nobody I was goin' 'cause I knew nobody woulda wanted to go with me anyway. It's been almost a year since it was dedicated, so like it was about time, you know. . . . But when I got to the Mall, well, I kinda got lost at first. Stumblin' all over the damn Monument grounds. Kept runnin' into all the wrong things. Fuckin' tourists and ducks and ponds and twisty paths and shit. But then finally: *boom.* There it was. Just over this one particular rise. And it was like a shock, you know. All gleaming in the sun. All stone-stiff and swept along the ground like the humongous wings of some damn dead airplane. Nose buried. Tail shot off and gone. And it really ain't all that crowded so I'm feelin' okay, you know. Kinda right, ready. . . . I make my way to one of them books under glass at one of the entrances. Flip through the pages, find Eddie's name. And that sends me to the right panel and line, see. And hey, what do you know? I mean like what do you fuckin' know? Like he's just got to be in the middle, right? Almost stone dead in the middle of the whole goddam thing. And I . . . I get up close, see. Stand right before it. And I read . . . I read: Edward A. Wallace, Jr.

[*Lifting his right hand.*]

I lift my right hand and it starts shakin', shakin' like a damn leaf. And somethin' starts turnin' upside down in my guts. But I don't stop.

[*Tracing the air.*]

'Cause I've gotta do it. I've gotta trace every single letter in my big brother's name. 'Cause I'm hopin' that maybe it'd be over then, finished, all this crazy-assed shit inside of me.

[*He stops tracing.*]

But it don't work. It don't fuckin' work.

[*He lets out a little laugh.*]

And you wanna know why? 'Cause all the while I'm doin' it I can fuckin' see myself, man.

[*He slowly begins backing upstage, away from "the wall."*]

See myself right there in that glassy stone wall. My reflection lookin' back at me lookin' back at those goddam small-assed little chiseled letters.

[*He pulls out the knife his brother left him.*]

Chiseled.

[*He raises the knife to his face and seems to be chiseling letters into his forehead as he speaks.*]

Edward A. Wallace, Jr. chiseled right across my own forehead.

[*He lowers the knife to his side.*]

No escape, Little Joe. No fuckin' escape."

LIVE BROADCAST
John William Schiffbauer

Dramatic
TOM, 20s

TOM POWERS, *a Hollywood movie star, explains to his agent,* JANE, *why, against her better judgment, he must participate in a live televised debate on a prime time political talk show.*

TOM   You know something, Jane? You are absolutely right. It is entirely about ego. And that's because most of the time guys like me are perceived as being spoiled, out of touch, and irresponsible jackasses. But I think you and I both know different. That's not who I am. I was born and raised on two hundred acres of the most beautiful farmland in Iowa, and my father and mother made damn sure that they instilled in me a sense of honor, duty, and integrity. But I been working this town going on three years now, and don't get me wrong, I love what I do, I love my job, and when I'm working I give it one hundred and ten percent. But I am more than just a pretty face on a one-sheet. I am intelligent, and I am articulate. I speak three languages, four, if we count English. And I went to a school which taught me that Art is more than just posing for the cover of *Vanity Fair*. I was taught that Art, in its best and brightest form, should be an expression of the human will, and of the human psyche, and that it should reflect reality. But you know what's the onion? That in the grand scheme of things, what does Art really matter, hm? Does it erase poverty? Feed the hungry? Clothe the naked? Create infrastructure? Ease the pain and suffering of those who are in pain and suffering? No. It doesn't. Not directly anyway. But you know what Art can do, though?

It can get people thinking. I can use my celebrity to help influence the debate instead of sitting comfortably on the sidelines like some sort of lame, chicken-ass wannabe whose only concern is how can I build a bigger house in Malibu Beach.

LOOKING AGAIN

Charles Evered

Comic
BILL, 20s to 30s

BILL *is in a bar with a male friend, giving him tips about how to pick up women.*

BILL   She wears a blouse like that because she wants to be able to see the extent to which you are able to keep yourself from lookin' at 'em. The point remains that the more you look at 'em, the less likely it'll be that you'll enjoy 'em someday. Be the cowboy, Steve. The cowboy doesn't look at 'em. The cowboy doesn't have to. You're supposed to be the cowboy. Used to be we'd cut down a tree and split it, throw some logs on the campfire, and stir up some grub. Now what are we? We are exactly what the eunuchs who run television shows depicted us into being. Marginalized metro-sexual tubs of butter incapable of threatening our own shadows. We are confused, confounded, passive, and compromised little toady boys. What are we? Are we men? Do men even really need to exist anymore? If they don't need our penises anymore to have a baby, if you don't even need to differentiate one gender from the other anymore, then why have two separate genders at all? Why don't we all just be one gender? Why don't we all just be a bunch of "Sam"s or "Terri"s—let's all cut our hair down just to the middle of our necks. Let's all wear pants or "chinos" or whatever the hell so-called men wear now. Why have pants at all, when you think of it—let's just have "leg coverings" so as not to offend those who don't feel comfortable wearing pants, and better yet, let's not wear clothes at all, as wearing them is in its own way discriminatory toward those who prefer not to so publicly declare their own gender. You want to be alive again, brother? You want to break the chains? Don't look at 'em.

LOOKING AGAIN
Charles Evered

Comic
BILL, 20s to 30s

BILL is in a bar with a male friend, giving him tips about how to pick up women, and about what you have to do these days to "be a man."

BILL   Steve, I don't want you to be offended by what I'm about to say to you, because you have to understand it isn't personal, and so I don't mean any offense to you directly. But I do want to say this: You are what this society calls a "man," but in millennia before us, let's be honest—you would be a liability. I want you to imagine what good you do—really take a long hard look at yourself. I'm not talking about feeling here, Steve—I'm talking about thinking. The world is falling apart because grown men don't know the difference anymore. People think because they feel something, it must be right. No doubt, Steve, you "feel" you are a good man. That you have some worth and that perhaps, someday, you will meet a woman of average attractiveness and perhaps above-average breast size and you'll couple with her and the two of you will roll around in an agreed-upon orgy of self-delusion that allows you both to believe you matter in the world. You'll mutually agree to subscribe to some made-up tenant of belief, and every Sunday you will go to church and act like something means something. Well, it doesn't Steve. It has no meaning. And neither do you. I want you to really think about what I'm about to propose to you—and I want you to think about it like a man would. I want you to think about taking your own life, because when all is said and done, it's the only real control we can exert upon a universe that otherwise has us reel-ing in anarchy and randomness. Seriously, think about it, Steve. And don't make a big production of it, either. If you're going to take your own life, do it in a way that would seem questionable as to whether you actually meant to do it at all. Do it with built-in plausible deniability so that your mother can tell her friends it was an "accident," or some kind of mishap, but for all that is right and true and good in this putrid world, Steve, do it.

LOVE SICK
Kristina Poe

Dramatic
CHRIS, 35

CHRIS *is at a group therapy session for the broken hearted, finally doing his step where he has to state clearly what happened and how he came to be in the group.*

CHRIS   [*Very uncomfortable.*] My name is Chris. I am here sharing with the group because my wife left me. I feel sad, and
lonely, but mostly what I feel is shame. Shame because I
was not man enough to hold on to my woman. And I know
that sounds caveman-ish, or whatever, but in my heart, I
know I am not a real man, because a real man would have
been able to keep her. A real man would have satisfied his
wife, so she didn't go looking for satisfaction elsewhere.
And not just sexual satisfaction, either, though that was
part of it—but financial and familial is just as important.
With me she lived in an apartment . . . with him she lives in
a two-story house with a pool and four kids . . . ALL boys,
even. So, I live with great shame knowing I am not a real
man. And other men know I'm not a real man . . . they have
proof—my wife left me. Well, first she cheated on me, and
left me . . . then came back to try and work it out when
the affair ended . . . but then, within two months she was
cheating on me again, with this Chester White. And then
she told me she loved me, but she was leaving me for that
guy. And she did . . . and six weeks later she was pregnant. I
don't hang out with my guy friends too much anymore, cuz
they know. They've been great, but they respect me a little
less; I can see it in their eyes. And it hurts. But what really
hurts, what is really almost unbearable is the mornings.

Because in the mornings, when I wake up, my mind is clear, and fresh, and for a few brief moments, I am the Man I used to be—happy and with his wife still in love with him . . . but then, at some point, usually about a minute later, my brain kicks on, and I remember that my life has turned upside down, and all of a sudden, I experience that devastation all over again, in full force. And it is crushing. And it's that moment, where I wonder if it's all worth it.

MANNING UP
Sean Christopher Lewis

Comic
RAYMOND, 35

RAYMOND *is talking to his best friend* DONNIE *in his Long Island Man Cave. The two men are terrified of the fact that they are both about to become fathers, and in this monologue* RAYMOND *describes his innate want to protect his wife from bullies she works with and his complete failure to do so.*

RAYMOND   Yeah. I mean she works harder than anyone I know. But of our friends and the like . . . she just, I see it. I see how important the place is to her. She's the goddam office manager and this guy j blames her for everything. And you know there's nothing I can do. I'm just power-less. And I keep thinking there's gotta be something I can do. Like I want to beat him up. So the shelter is in this old church, right. Like 1800s or something—I mean the build-ing's falling apart—and it's Sally's job to keep things run-ning. So, she calls me one day in tears. And I've had it, like with this guy, I'm gonna look his address up and I'm going to tear him a new one . . . and Sally says, have you looked outside? And I say, yeah. And she says it's raining. And she just breaks down. And I'm like, what's going on? And she says it's raining in the meeting room. The roof has a break in it . . . like this big . . . [*Demonstrates with hands.*] . . . and water's just pouring in. And they already had the roofers in once and she just keeps crying because she knows this guy is going to blame her . . . So I got in my car and drove over there and I don't know what I'm doing. I bought a bunch of caulk and it was like *The A-Team*. She met me at the door and I had these caulk guns and this caulk and I think it was for glass but whatever—she says, "You made it." And it's like an old Bogart movie. She's got that look in her eyes, you know, "Help me." I mean usually it's me that has that look. But I love it . . . And I say, "Yeah, I'm gonna take care of this. Don't you worry. I'm gonna take care of it good." So I get up there and it's a mess. Water's coming down the roof, it's not getting drained, I'm so drenched my clothes weigh as much as I do. And I start to caulk everything. I'm caulking walls, the ceiling, inside the ceiling, it's just everywhere, I'm using electrical tape to hold it all in. And she's watching me and some of the families are coming in looking. Luckily, it's no one else. I DON'T KNOW WHAT THE HELL I'M DO-ING, MAN. I'm a complete fraud, basically. All I know is that ceiling right now has about forty pounds of caulk in it. And I signed the inside of it "Jeremy"—her boss—"can suck it, signed Sally Guinness's husband."

A MEASURE OF CRUELTY
Joe Calarco

Seriocomic
DEREK, teens

After committing a heinous bullying crime, DEREK, *a troubled teen has been sheltered by a bar owner who is wrestling with demons of his own.* DEREK *feels safe and feels he can confide in the older man.*

DEREK   I couldn't even get a dog. When I was eight I wanted a dog—you know, a man's best friend kinda situation—but he was like, "No way. I'm not picking up after some stanky-ass dog. I gotta do enough of that with you." And he was like, "And I don't care how much you promise me you'll do it yourself. You never do anything you say you're gonna do, and I'm not having dog shit stinking up my house 'cause my son's a lazy fuck up." I got all upset, and I guess that must've made him all marshmallowy inside for a split second 'cause he was all, "Stop crying like a little girl. Shut up, and I'll buy you a hamster," which was like the first and last time he ever gave me anything. And he was all, "Keep it in your room, 'cause when you forget to clean up after it, you're the one who'll have to deal with the stanky-ass cage." So he minivanned my ass over to the pet store and I said to the clerkage all standing around, I said, "I got a name picked out: Bruno. Go get me Bruno the hamster." And they brought me out the most Bruno-looking hamster you ever seen. We took him home and like a week later, thwack, thwack, thwack, Bruno pops out some babies. And I was like, "Why'd they tell me it was a boy when it was really a girl?" That was like the first "the world sucks" kinda lie that ever happened to me. But I thought, "Okay, maybe one of them babies can be my Bruno the Second." And I was hanging over the cage peaking in, trying to get a look at which one I was gonna pick, and I noticed this tiny little one, like the mayor of mini-McHamsterville. And it was laying on its side all gasping for breath and stuff. And then his mama? Dude, she started eating him. I'm not bullshitting you. I tried to stop it. I was screaming and shaking the cage, but the more I did, the faster she ate. And my dad came in bitching at me to shut up, and then he saw what I was screaming about, and he smiled and said, "Don't worry. That's just her mothering instinct or whatever kicking in." He told me that if one of her babies is too weak she'll eat it knowing it won't survive this world, so it's like her saving her baby from a monumentally shitty life. He was all, "Gotta be strong or you'll get eaten alive. That's what she's teaching her other pups. What she's doing right there? That's for them. That's what love is." Douchebag thing to say, right?

A MEASURE OF CRUELTY

Joe Calarco

Seriocomic
DEREK, teens

*After committing a heinous bullying crime, DEREK, a troubled
teen, is sheltered by a bar owner who is wrestling with demons of
his own. DEREK confides in the older man while munching on a
strawberry Pop-Tart.*

DEREK   I'm not bullshitting you. It was just like in that movie
with all those Nazis burned up trying to steal all of God's
power. Even with just that sliver of a window back there,
I could see it and I was thinking, "What if it stayed like
this?" Like wake up to sizzle, sizzle, bang, bang, flash.
Havin' to pull shades at night for even a chance a shut-
eye. Storing up on Tylenol PM. Get you all dopey. You
start slipping into some just-before-dreamtime state and
flash, flash, flash! Flying out of bed wondering where
all the paparazzi came from. Stumble to the bathroom
and suck down some Nyquil. Fall face first back into your
mattress and pow, pow, pow! All those flashes again. But
you're so whacked out on over-the-counter-type sleeping aids that all you can do is roll over and reach for some
eye-lubrication-type action making sure all the red's out,
making yourself all pretty. Hell, everybody's doing it. We're
talking major Visine shortage. Whole cities full of people
draggin' ass out onto the front lawns to watch the light
show—forgettin' to feed the kids, lettin' the house go to
hell. Screw the sofa. Let Fido go to town. Dogs chompin'
down on cushion stuffing, shit stains on the shiny new
shag. I'm tellin' you everyone's just gonna be loungin' in
a lawn chair, twenty-four hours, three hundred sixty-five

days, starin' up, up, up at the flash, flash, boom. Nobody carin' about nothin' no more. Fruit rotting in the grocery stores. Supermarkets stinkin' a sour milk. Nobody buying nothin'. Who needs Lean Cuisine? Just lean right over, grab a hunk a grass from the green, green lawn, munchin' down on weedage, snackin' on some snails, starin' up, up, up, smiling. Everybody thinking God sent down some kind of host of angels to snap a family portrait, you know? I am like totally addicted to this strawberry poptartification.

MIDDLEMEN
David Jenkins

Seriocomic
MICHAEL, mid- to late 20s

MICHAEL AARONSON *is exhausted and his nerves are worn. Normally a truthful and trusting person, he has found himself complicit in the bankrupting of Bolivia, and fears the consequences. This monologue is addressed directly to the audience.*

MICHAEL   I don't sleep. [*Beat.*] Not anymore, not lately. [*Beat.*] It's not by choice. I *like* sleep, it's not . . . a boycott or anything. [*Beat.*] I doze. Can't remember the last time I had a good night's . . . When I used to sleep, I would dream of numbers. Peaceful dreams (I love numbers). I dream of other things, too, but the ones I remember the most vividly are math based. It's just, lately I . . . I haven't been able to shut my mind off. Listen, we're all adults here, right? We know that everything . . . you know . . . in *business* . . . operates on a sort of flexibility. We're all adults, we know that. Why should my job be any different? I'm not, uh, not immune to the laws of physics. I know that sometimes you have to make a deficit look like a surplus, or move a decimal point here or there. [*Beat.*] You get numbers on their own, in their natural habitat, and they're fine. But you put them in the hands of human beings . . . Things Mean Things. You know? [*Beat.*] I know I'm being vague. Uh, coffee cup here [*Picking up a mug.*] will always mean coffee cup. You can smash it, and it turns into porcelain shards, or smash it further until it's just dust, but as long as it's in this form, this will always equal coffee cup. It doesn't equal cat, or car. Do you, do you know . . . ? (Okay, just bear with me here. This sort of thing might be why I'm still single.) Uh, all through our lives, all around us, we have these, uh, *facts*, I guess. This is my hand, not my foot. Okay, check, I know that, I'm never going to have to be reminded of that again, I can go on with my life, and never doubt that information. And that's numbers. These are *things* . . . they're . . . they're *facts*. And I'm in the position a lot of times of being asked to say that a coffee cup is a cat, and, and, I . . . Long story short, I may have bankrupted Bolivia.

THE MOTHERF**KER WITH THE HAT
Stephen Adly Guirgis

Seriocomic
BOBBY, 30s

BOBBY, *an ex-con, lives with his girlfriend,* VERONICA. *He has been trying to get his life back together, going to AA meetings, etcetera, but then he comes home and finds a man's hat in their room. He thinks it belongs to a guy who lives downstairs. Here, he tells his cousin,* JULIO, *how he got even with the guy.*

BOBBY   Anyway, Veronica, I think, was upset about the AA woman even though for all she knows nothing happened, and so, my belief is she started fuckin' the motherfucker with the hat so she could prove to herself that she don't love me, but, of course, we all know she do love me, but now, I found out about it cuz the motherfucker left his hat on my table—so—I got upset, I got a gun from Chuchi, and I took the hat and the gun to the motherfucker with the hat's apartment downstairs, and . . . that's when a incident happened. All I did: I knocked on the door. Motherfucker with the hat answered. I didn't say nothing. I just took the hat—the hat from my house, tossed it on his carpet, stared him straight in the eye, cocked the gun, and shot the fuckin' hat on the carpet. Dass all I did. I shot his hat. Dass all. And—BELIEVE ME—the motherfucker *knew* what that was about! The problem is, the bullet went through his hat, ricko-shayed off his floor, blew out his big-screen TV, and put a hole into the guy next door's apartment who was home at the time, so, I had to, like, flee . . . And now I gotta return the gun to fuckin' Chuchi, but he ain't around, so could you please hide the fuckin' gun until, like, Chuchi could be located, please?

THE MOTHERF**KER WITH THE HAT
Stephen Adly Guirgis

Dramatic
COUSIN JULIO, 30s

JACKIE, *an ex-con, has recently learned that his AA sponsor has been screwing his girlfriend,* VERONICA. *He has asked his cousin,* JULIO, *to help him confront the guy.* JULIO *tells* JACKIE *exactly what he thinks of him first.*

COUSIN JULIO   The reason I said I'm doing this more for
your mother's memory than for you is because, maybe
I never said this before, but, I don't like you very much.
And the reason I don't like you very much is because you
think you're a nice guy, but really Jackie, you're not that
nice. You've basically made fun of me my whole life, you
talk a lot of shit, you fuck people over—not all the time
but sometimes—and really, the space between who you
think you are and who you actually are is a pretty embar-
rassingly wide gap. I hope this AA thing works out for
you. Because the cousin I loved and hung out with and
played Booties Up with when I was eight—he bears no
resemblance to the *cabroncito* I'm looking at right now.
When I first came to the States from PR, you had my back,
and, really, you were a hero to me. And now, *Dios perdona*,
the hero is a zero, *mijo*! My Marisol was right about you:
It's always about Jackie. We've been married three years
now, and whenever you come by our home, you don't
even bring so much as a bag of pistachios. And yet, you
see nothing wrong with jeopardizing my relationship and
my apartment and our safety by bringing criminal things
like this caca into our home. You're not a good friend, and
you're not a good relative. My Marisol called it: You're a

user. But thass okay. And that's all I got to say on that, so you can get out of my apartment now, and go do all those very more important things than spending time with you cousin Julio, okay?

NEVA
Guillermo Calderón
(translation by Andrea Thome)

Dramatic
ALEKO, 30

ALEKO, an actor, declares his love for OLGA, *his company's leading lady whose husband, the playwright* ANTON CHEKHOV, *has recently died.*

ALEKO   Olga, I'm a scab. I didn't have shoes until I was thirteen years old. I drank milk from my mother's and my sister's breasts, and only when they had babies. My father beat me, I never saw him sober and he never looked me in the eye. A priest raised me in his home because he said I knew how to sing and because in the winter I didn't cry from hunger.

That's how life was in the country, Olga, and it was beautiful. I wanted to live in the city, but when I got here I saw how some drunks beat a horse to death. I bent down, kissed its eyes and I got stained with blood, Olga. Just like you, stained with blood. That's why when I went to see you at the theater, invited by a woman who paid me to love her, I fell in love with you. Because you are sad, because you appear older than you are, because you know how to walk, because I would like to be like that and dress like that. And since you came to rehearse with us I've had a constant erection. For the last two weeks I've been urinating in the street, my penis freezes, it turns black. I'd love . . . to penetrate you. I love you and I want you to love me, but you won't love me because I'm poor. Don't let my soldier's face mislead you, when I'm naked you'll realize. That's how we poor people are—we have fewer bones and the few that we have are bigger, we're lopsided. I have rat bites on my buttocks. I smell like a woman where I ought to smell like a man and I don't know how to love without wanting to hit, kill, vomit, pray, drink, and love some more. The most important organ in my body is my appendix and I want to stick it in your kidney and watch you sweat.

NIGHTNIGHT
Lucas Hnath

Dramatic
TOM, 20s to 30s

TOM *is an astronaut on a space shuttle, here describing a terrible recurring dream.*

TOM   I sleep all night now, but when I sleep, it's all nightmares. Terrible nightmares, nightmares about the space walk. Every night, same nightmare, where I'm out there in the suit and the tether breaks. In the dream, I never see how it breaks or why it breaks, but that's what happens, every time: the tether breaks, and I try to grab on to the edge of the ship but I miss and I just keep going farther and farther away from the spacecraft. And my suit is equipped with a nitrogen blast. And I fire it and hope that it sends me back in the direction of the spacecraft. But every time it either doesn't fire or it misfires or it fires but it fires in the wrong direction. And so I keep floating because there's nothing to stop me. But I have my radio, and I have about forty-five minutes of oxygen left in my primary tank, and I can hear Mission Control and they can hear me. And the people on Earth, in Mission Control, they can patch me through to maybe a girlfriend or something. And I try calling but she doesn't pick up. So I try calling one of the other girlfriends, but she's not home. And I ask Mission Control to play me a song or something, but in the dream, they don't have any of the music that I like, and so I sit in silence and look around and I can see the stars, and the stars look different because all I have is a thin visor between me and the stars and I can see what starlight really looks like and real starlight is all sorts of colors like red and purple and blue.

And when my forty-five minutes of oxygen run out, I have a choice: I can let them run out or I can switch to my secondary tank, and that will give me another two hours and I can use that extra time to call my mother and say good-bye or I could just keep drifting off and looking at the stars, but whether or not I switch to those secondary tanks, either way, eventually, the oxygen will run out. And when it runs out, it runs out gradually. And when it runs out, I start to feel myself fading, my vision becomes hazy, and the one sun looks like two blurry suns. And I look at our spacecraft, and the spacecraft now looks like a tiny white speck, a small point of light, way far away, but a "far away" that seems sort of close and easy to get to, except I'm too tired to try, and that feels good, because that's how the brain tells you to feel in moments like this, that's how—and I feel sleepy, and I feel slow, and I feel hazy, and I feel nice. And then my brain shuts off. And soon after, so do I. And then that's when I wake up.

NORTH TO MAINE
Brenton Lengel

Dramatic
NICK, 27

NICK *is hiking the Appalachian Trail with* ADAM, *who is seeking an adventure along the lines of the Fellowship of the Ring but so far hasn't found it.* NICK *explains to him that, in fact, he has.*

NICK   There are no wizards or orcs, but look: you are having your adventure . . . do you believe in God? Well I don't, and I figure we're better off without him. It's like what Nietzsche said: In a universe without God, our lives have no inherent meaning, other than what we impose. We are the ones who make our lives great; WE take the chaos around us and mold it into something beautiful. That's what you're doing. You are on an adventure . . . that doesn't change because there are no dragons or wizards. Hell, if you ask me, you're better off without them. There's more magic in these hills, or in Picasso, or Einstein, than in all the fairies or gods ever imagined. You're an über-nerd, but you're an über-nerd who's living life on his terms, and I think that's pretty fucking cool. That drama with your parents? It's fucked up, but you know what? It's going to pass. Things are going to get easier. That's the way life is. It's like climbing a goddamn mountain. You haul your ass up the switchbacks until your clothes are caked with salt, and your eyes are burning and blurry from the sweat, and your legs are getting ready to mutiny. You keep telling yourself that the summit is right around the next corner . . . and it's not, but you'll get there eventually. And no matter how bad it seems, and how much your muscles scream for you to stop, you can always take one more step. And when you

get there, man . . . you look out over the hills and the val-
leys and if it's clear enough, it's like you can see forever;
like you can see through time. And the future and past are
stretched out before you in all directions, and you say to
yourself, "I climb mountains."

ONE NIGHT
Charles Fuller

Dramatic
HORACE: late 20s, African American

HORACE *has been looking out for* ALICIA, *a woman with whom he served in Iraq who was raped there by three men, two of whom she was able to identify, but the army dismissed her charges against them. The two of them are homeless. The shelter where they were staying burned down and they are now in a seedy motel room. Here,* HORACE *reveals why he has been trying to save* ALICIA. *He was the third man.*

HORACE   Started as a *joke,* that's all! You have to *come down* from killing people every day—break the monotony of every hour—every minute!—You have to—to *fuck something!*—Get it out of you! We wanted to—snatch some of that *smart-mouth* from you and McCray! We did all the *killing,* but you two got *commendations* for driving up in a fucking gun truck? That was our third day under fire, and not one grunt from A platoon got anything but put down because of a *bitch sergeant* and her *bitch shotgun*! You shouldn't have been there in the first place! [*Pauses, annoyed with himself.*] I was in it—and—but Frank and Terry said they wouldn't go unless we went all the way—an' *I had to participate*! It was *my joke*! Every day, *everywhere*—after all the bodies I left rotting in the Sandbox your face that one night was all I could see—I thought if I could find you—I—I would give you money—beg your forgiveness and "walk off down range" . . . but you were homeless—helpless—and *so beautiful*—I decided to stay for a minute—run interference for you, lead the way, eliminate the *enemy*—like I did in the Sandbox [*Slight pause.*] I hoped you'd forget—I'm so sorry! I tried, Alicia [*Pause.*] . . . I tried! I kept the whole *world* off you, Sarge! *I* took down the woman at the VA, when you needed somebody to speak up for you! Who got the shelter at Ninety-three-thirteen? *I* made sure you could march through the mess of the application papers and your disability claims. *I* eliminated everything in your path—but the apartment was different, wasn't it? Where would *I* be once you got it? It was all for Louis! Who needs Horace then? Well, without me you're *nobody-nothing-nowhere*—understand?

THE OTHER FELIX
Reina Hardy

Comic
THE OTHER FELIX, late 20s to early 30s

FELIX BETTLEMAN *is a professional gambler and a recent victim of identity theft. But the thief is after more than* FELIX's *name and credit rating—he's after* FELIX's *soul. In this monologue, the* OTHER FELIX *leaves a phone message for* FELIX's *ex-girlfriend* LILY *in an attempt to further assimilate his identity by winning her love.*

THE OTHER FELIX   Sir? Sir? Can I talk to you for a second? Sir? Sir? You can't play blackjack here anymore. . . . You're kidding me. I just lost thousands of dollars- . . . You can't play blackjack You must- . . . Surely you jest! I lost I just lost you must be kidding . . . Sir, you can't- . . . You can't You can't possibly mean that. I just lost thousands of dollars! Surely you're kidding! . . . I'm serious. . . . Oh well, um, so it goes. I mean really it's the same old song, just the same exchange between me who remains more or less constant with certain tweaks and innovations here and there and a slew of different characters of, you know, varying mettle, so this this gentleman's mettle was not the toughest or scariest I had encountered. On the other hand I felt guilty about being kind of obnoxious, because I mean really he was civil and there was no need to be. I just *had* lost thousands of dollars and was kind of sad and emotive which is, as they say in poker, showing weakness and no damn good. Anyway, I'm in Mississippi, where I am having the dickens of a time getting down. They don't like the action anywhere. And despite the fact that they win, every time I walk into a casino. I mean. Why do they bother to chase me out? I'm perplexed. These and other quandaries, as well as the ongoing question of where is Lily Arkidner, preoccupy me. I wake up dreaming about you and go to sleep the same way and I can't wait to see you next week and yeah so I miss you is implicit in all this and also a fact and goodnight goodnight.

THE OTHER FELIX
Reina Hardy

Dramatic
FELIX, late 20s to early 30s

FELIX BETTLEMAN is a professional gambler, and a recent victim of identity theft. But the thief is after more than FELIX's name and credit rating. He wants FELIX's entire life, including his ex-girlfriend, LILY ARKIDNER. In this monologue, FELIX chases after the OTHER FELIX in an attempt to stop him from harming LILY.

FELIX So I get into the car, and I go north. Like a compass. And always, just before me Just under the horizon there is a powder-blue Mustang convertible that I never see. What a jerk, to drive a convertible when you need to keep the hood up. It's like an insult to weather and to convertibles. I know because I've done it. It's cold—the air smells sharp like New Year's Day. There are great silent trees and as the car makes low buzzing turns they sift snow down on my roof and it looks like the sound of bells. They have auroras up here. I mean, not right now but there could be one at any moment and you sort of live with that knowledge like the knowledge that at any moment you could turn the corner and jam your fenders into a light blue Mustang convertible with the hood up, and you'd both drift into a snowbank like lovers. Somehow it gets mixed up in my mind with the aurora borealis so that if one happens the other will happen, and if one doesn't happen neither will. Either I crash into a bank of powder-blue light or I drive through the dark and the silent sound of bells forever and ever. And as I drive I am always about to think of you and really, it's no different than the last time I was here when I thought of you at every moment and I wanted to see the

111

northern lights and I never did. The sky above is deep and black, and then it's filled with snow. For no reason, I say a word out loud. Angel. And then there is a hard white flutter and something unfolds across my windshield and I do crash without his help all-by-my-Felix and I think, "Fuck. I have conjured up some kind of justice and now here I die" as the car glides in a slow circle and nestles itself by the embankment, like parallel parking itself in a bag of marshmallows. I turn up, not-dead and the angel of justice is just a large piece of white paper that had not seemed previously important and that had unfolded its wide white self as soon as my unconscious finger flicked the windshield wipers at the first sight of snow. It's a message. It's a town. It's an address. It's a hotel number. It's not far. And then it happened. The sky just—exploded. And I am looking right at an aurora. It's that thing I was waiting for. He must be looking at it too.

PALOMA
Anne García-Romero

Dramatic
IBRAHIM, late 20s

IBRAHIM *tells his friend about his father's reaction when he found out* IBRAHIM *is dating a girl who is not a Muslim.*

IBRAHIM   I needed some space so I left the hotel, walked around for a while and then decided to take the Metro to Sol. I walked out of the station and up the stairs of this Internet and phone place. I paid five euros for booth six and dialed, knowing my pop would be home, watching some shit on the History channel. I needed some space so I went out for a walk and decided to call my father. I sat in that booth sweating, my stomach turning, my intestines cramping, my bladder aching, fight or flight, you know? . . . And that fucking phone kept ringing and ringing. But he picked up, eventually. And I'm like, "Yo, pop." And he's like, [*With slight Moroccan accent.*] "What the hell are you doing calling me at one thirty in the morning in Madrid?" And I'm like, "I wanted to chat with you." And then I'm starting to sound like I'm real nervous, you know? At first I was like talking small talk and shit and I knew my pop was getting pissed. [*With slight Moroccan accent.*] "What, you run out of money?" And I'm like, "No, pop. I . . . I met someone." And he's like, [*With slight Moroccan accent.*] "You get a girl pregnant and I'll kick your ass." And I'm like, "Pop. Her name is Paloma." And he's like, [*With slight Moroccan accent.*] "You meet a nice Muslim girl with a Spanish name?" And I'm like, "She's nice. She has a Spanish name. But she's not Muslim." And he's like, [*With slight Moroccan accent.*] "What about *Sharzad*?" The woman at the mosque my father wanted me to marry. And I'm like,

"Pop. I'm not seeing her anymore." And he's like, [*With slight Moroccan accent.*] "Your mother and I know." And then my stomach starts to fuckin' ache and I have to shit real bad and I'm like fuck, I know that tone in his voice. He's like, [*With slight Moroccan accent.*] "She called us three days ago. She told us you went to Madrid with your new girlfriend. She told us her name is Paloma. She told us she is Christian." And he proceeded to cuss me out real rapid fire in Arabic, you know. I didn't know shit what he was saying but the energy was serious and I was like fuck. And then in like his intense English he says things like, [*With slight Moroccan accent.*] "You know, God will punish you for your sins and our family's reputation is ruined."

THE PATRON SAINT OF SEA MONSTERS
Marlane Gomard Meyer

Dramatic
CALVIN, 20s to 30s

CALVIN *is on trial for killing his wife,* MARIE. *He is explaining it all to the judge.*

CALVIN Those bones in the sack, are her bones. Till I saw those bones I wasn't sure I would be able to turn myself in. Not being the kind of man who owns up to his mistakes. But when I saw those bones . . . I remembered, what a pretty girl she had been. How lively and sassy. And how much I loved her. [*Beat.*] We were happy for a while, like kids are. But then I couldn't keep a job. Marie got fed up and decided to go to beauty school. When she went to apprentice in another town she started to have a life there, started to have new friends. She said all the men she worked with were gay but I didn't believe her. So one day I showed up at her job, drunk, got into a fight with this guy and broke his jaw. That tore it. She said she wanted a divorce. I said, fine! I let her pack up. She kissed me good-bye and she started to cry and I thought for a minute there she'd changed her mind but . . . she got in her car and drove away. I watched her, I waved. But . . . I knew she'd be back because I'd taken her license and registration! [*Smiles.*] I had it all planned out, how I was gonna win her back. I bought a good, used, suit—got my hair professionally styled. And I borrowed money to buy her a nice ring. We'd just had a simple gold band when we got married . . . I wanted to get her a diamond. So, I went to the place where my half brother, Jack, worked, and he helped me pick out a beautiful ring. Big, shiny, and surprisingly inexpensive, which should have tipped me off. I thought she'd come home pretty quick, but it took three whole days. So that when she finally did come back, pissed as shit, instead of seeing me looking sharp, she saw me drunk, in an old dirty suit. But what I saw was worse. I saw that same dead-eyed, disappointed look my ma has when she sees me. But, being drunk, I thought I still had a chance. I pulled out the ring and showed her and she looked at it and she started laughing. Jack had sold me a zircon—if you don't know what that is, it's a fake god-damned diamond. She could tell right away and she started in on how stupid I was and how she was glad to be rid of me. And it was there, in that great darkness between what I had dreamed of and how that dream was sailing down the shit hole that I became lost, which I think is why I grabbed her by the neck and held on like I did. Or maybe it was be-cause I did not want to be alone again. Do you understand? Because if there is one way to keep a woman with you forever, it is to take the life she's going to live without you.

POLLYWOG

John P. McEneny

Dramatic
GUNTHER, 20

GUNTHER JORBENADZE, _who teaches swimming at a Christian
high school, tells how his family was massacred in the Republic
of Georgia._

GUNTHER   We knew the separatists were coming so my
mother hid me in closet on the top shelf. I was small and
made myself smaller. Nekulai ran to get my father who I
think was still in the quarry. I had never seen my mother
so scared. She didn't want to go anywhere until my father
was back. There was a UN cease-fire so my father felt safe
to leave us alone. And then the men came and they told
her to take off all of her clothes and she started screaming.
And I put my fists together in that dark shelf and I prayed to
God. When I had my first communion—I remember kneel-
ing on hard wood pew, talking to God in my head like he
was some pal that could answer. "Thank you God for my
parents, my new blue sneakers, and could you help make
my dog feel better. Your friend, Gunther." And then in that
closet while my mother wept in her own kitchen—I prayed
again—more than I ever had before. "Please God, make
these men go away. Don't let my mother cry. Don't let them
hurt her. Don't let them do to me what they were doing
to her." And then I heard my father and Nekulai run in and
there was screaming and more pounding. I waited in the
closet praying to God again. One last time: "Please make
my family be all right. Please don't let me have to open the
door, climb down, and see them dead. Please don't make
me see my mother naked crying with shaking hands over

my bleeding brother. Please don't make me see my father dead on the floor with his eyes still open. Please God." But God doesn't listen to my prayers. And if he did, he said: "I don't care, Gunther." So I know there's no God. At least there's no God that day. Not in Sukhumi.

PRINCES OF WACO
Robert Askins

Dramatic
JIM, 20

JIM's daddy was a preacher. He preached in Texas. JIM's daddy died. JIM is having trouble keeping it together. Somebody who isn't too smart asked him to speak at the funeral. To speak to a congregation whose secrets he knows and whose lies he hates. This is what he says.

JIM   I ain't wanna be here. I didn't wanna come but somebody . . . and Deacon Bradley saw me passin' by and well . . . That's how come I'm dressed like this . . . I don't know how to do this. Seein' everybody out there all teary-eyed. All respectful. I don't . . . okay . . . He was a smart man. I can say that about him. 'Cause that's what we're supposed to do. Right? Say the good stuff. He was a smart man. He spoke with the voice of God . . . 'cause . . . 'cause . . . Fuck it. Why can't we be honest.

Here in front of God why can't we be honest. I know where he hid his porn. He wanted to kill someone in Vietnam. He hated potato salad . . . all of your potato salad . . . He spoke with the voice of God 'cause it let him tell us all what pieces of shit we are. And we are. Brothers and sisters we are. Half of you have fucked Bill Fischer's wife. And everybody knows it. Everybody. This is what he saw sitting in these pews. Lust. Gluttony. Greed. Who won't Jim Kettler kill for a dollar. Ronnie Todd beats the shit outta his kids every Saturday and he comes here to get saved every Sunday.

[*Jim bows his head. He raises it again.*]

He wept in the night for a better world. He wept and wept and wept and in the morning Jesus come to him and whispered in his ear: You save your water. JESUS WANTED YOU TO.

120

RADIANCE

Cusi Cram

Dramatic
ROB, 30s

ROB was the copilot on the Enola Gay, the plane that dropped the A-bomb on Hiroshima. He is in Hollywood to appear on a segment of the television show This Is Your Life, *but he has fled the studio when he learned that also on the program will be the Hiroshima Maidens, women who were horribly disfigured by the bomb. He has come into a dive bar near the studio. Here, he is talking to* MAY, *the cocktail waitress, about a dangerous incident that occurred before he became a member of the Enola Gay's crew.*

ROB   I was always partial to more poetic names. I felt like if I was gonna go down in flames I wanted to be floating on something that wasn't the punch line of a joke. My favorite one was *The Majestic*. And she was just that. Not flying her made me nervy already. And then, right before I go, my colonel tells me my regular navigator won't be coming with me. And to a pilot that's kinda like telling you your wife won't be coming with you on your honeymoon. So, I get into the cockpit with van Kirk, this annoying navigator, good at his job but a sour little prick. And I'm sitting on the runway in *The Great Artiste*, on what very well could be my last mission of the war, and I watch *Straight Flush* slip into the air, nice and easy. Same for my buddy Captain Bock's plane, *Bock's Car*—another joke name. The plane ahead of me was called *Strange Cargo*. Just as she approached the runway, this grating sound started coming from her. And just like that, her bomb bay doors flew open! The pilot just slammed on his breaks and a ten thousand pound, bright orange blockbuster bomb lands right there on the runway.

A few hundred feet from me and my crew. And I'm thinking to myself, this is how it's gonna end? Talk about a joke. Me and my crew had to stay put, not move an inch. And that's when I started singing, "London Bridge Is Falling Down." The song just came out of my mouth and before I know it the whole crew is singing with me.

[*Singing.*]

"Build it up with Japs and Krauts. Japs and Krauts. Japs and Krauts . . ." We were singing like stupid kids while we watched firemen cover that bomb in foam. And we kept on singing when a crew of soldiers put shackles around that thing and winched it up, inch by inch. Took hours. They treated that bomb like it was the finest crystal.

RAVISHED
Don Nigro

Dramatic
COLL, 20s

In this modern retelling of the tale William Shakespeare told in The Rape of Lucrece, COLL, *a young man, works for a privately contracted company in a war in a far-off place and has been seriously scarred emotionally by his experiences there. Here, he sits before a fire in the night in that war zone and talks to his fellow worker* JOHN TARQUIN *about his girl back home,* LUCRECE.

COLL   I close my eyes and try to picture her. I have the photograph, but it's not like her. I mean, it is, but it isn't. It's just one piece of her. One expression on her face, but her face is always different. Her eyes change color in the light. Do you know how when you're with someone you love, it's hard to focus on them? It's like they always somehow get away from you before you can really touch them. Even when you're touching them sometimes you can't really see them because you're so close. You can only see part of them. You can only touch part of them. And then they're gone, and you try to remember, but you can't quite. Not enough. Not clearly enough. They're just these half-remembered fragments in your head, and you can't be satisfied until you see them again. But then perhaps you don't. At some point, you don't. Any time could be the last time. Maybe you know it is, and maybe you don't. I don't want to forget anything. I want to remember all of her, every inch of her flesh. I want to remember how it felt to kiss every part of her. Her lips were soft and full. Her breasts. The moment when she'd uncover her breasts. It was always this miraculous thing. Kissing her. Kissing her stomach. Kissing her back. The way her back tapers down to her waist. Her arms. She has the most beautiful arms. The down on her arms. Her hands. The way she sculpts the air with her hands when she's excited, when she's talking, her hands seem to take on a life of their own. It's like poetry. The way her hands move. I don't want to forget. If I say the words, I won't forget.

She would make this little noise. When I entered her. This very strange little murmur of something like surprise. Fear. Pleasure. Pain. I don't know what exactly it was, but it was an astonishingly erotic thing. And then she'd cry. While we were making love. She'd sob like a child. I don't know why she cried. She wouldn't tell me. I suppose she didn't know. Or maybe she knew, and didn't think it was any of my business. She was a stranger to me, really. The more we made love, the stranger she got. At first I'd be concerned, but then something in me would just take over and it didn't matter, and she was everything and then she'd kind of disappear. And then when it was over, she'd hold onto me, but she wouldn't look at me. But then finally she would look at me, into my eyes, as if she was trying to remember who I was. As if I was the stranger. It always scared the crap out of me. I just wanted to get away from her. I suppose it was guilt. As if I'd done something terrible to her. As if I'd violated her, somehow. But then the lust would come again. She'd be sitting there naked on the bed, with her arms around her legs, her face resting against her knees, looking so small and helpless and lost, as if somebody had just done something so terrible to her that nothing could ever make it right again. And then I'd feel the lust rising up in me again. And I'd kiss her back and run my hands along her arms and kiss her hair, kiss her neck, and she'd stay curled up tight, not letting me in. Not letting me in. She never let me in.

THE RECOMMENDATION
Jonathan Caren

Seriocomic
DWIGHT: late 20s to early 30s, African American

DWIGHT *is in a small holding cell at a jail in Hollywood, talking to cellmate ADAM FELDMAN, who has never been in such a hell-hole and has no idea why he has been brought there by the cops. DWIGHT tells ADAM why he has been arrested this time. DWIGHT has a hyperactive fantasy life, and one of his fantasies is that he and Steven Spielberg are buddies.*

DWIGHT   You know Spielberg? That's my boy. *E.T., Indiana Jones, Ghostbusters* shit. You like that movie? That's some funny-ass shit, right? So check it out. I'm chilling up in my Hollywood bungalow, kicking it, me and Steven, and this muthafuckin' cop shows up. I know! I'm just minding my own business, *howling it up in my bowling alley*, and he says he's gotta talk to me. At first I'm like racking my brain at what's he's talking about, and then I remember the Korean woman. The muthafuckin' Korean woman. This is over a *year* ago at the 76 on La Cienaga and Venice. I'm with this sweet-ass model from the Ukraine, you know, like one of them fashion runway models and shit, no joke. We about to go to dinner up at Mr. Chow's but my Bentley's running outta premium and Mr. Belvedere ain't driving me this week 'cause he's on vacation in the Caribbean. So I pull in, got my boy R. Kelly on the stereo and go to pay in cash, 'cause I'm doing alright, you know, gots me some money now. I hand the [Korean] bitch a fifty. Say, "Fill me up on three." I go back, start fillin' my tank, but Bentley only fills like halfway. I go back to the Korean. I say, "Yo, somethin' wrong with your machine 'cause it only fillin' me up like twenty." And she says, [*with a Korean accent*] "You give me twenny." I say, "Hell no, I gave you *fifty*. Check yo' register," so either bitch be scammin' me or she hid fifty so good now she cant's find it. I got my girl, I'm planning on spending that money on a primo bottle of Dom, but the chink won't give me my shit back. So instead of going ghetto, I have this Evian I be sippin' on. Just let it go in her direction. Wash her window clean so she can see shit better, know what I'm sayin'? But Korean calls the cops . . . So now I'm just waiting on Spielberg, 'cause he's gonna come on out here and sort all this shit out.

THE RECOMMENDATION
Jonathan Caren

Comic
DWIGHT: late 20s to early 30s, African American

DWIGHT *is in a small holding cell at a jail in Hollywood, talking to cellmate* ADAM FELDMAN, *who has never been in such a hellhole and has no idea why he has been brought there by the cops.* ADAM *is a personal assistant to a Hollywood producer, and* DWIGHT *decides this is a golden opportunity to pitch a movie idea he has.*

DWIGHT   I got a movie idea. This is some real blockbuster box-office shit! You wanna hear my movie idea or not? OK, if you insist. It's called *Alien Trash Man*. See—homeboy gets kicked out of Earth. Fucking twenty-eight-dollar car stereo holdup, know what I'm saying? The people on Earth send him up to this planet to get rid of him. But when he gets there, all them peoples are in like gold capes and wearing Versace eye patches. But since he's like, *normal* guy, they call him the alien and make him haul out trash. Every morning, he comes by five a.m. to collect their trash from their futuristic homes 'cause he's the *Alien Trash Man*. They be treatin' him like some lower species and shit. Then one day, he opens up the trashes to see what they all be throwin' out and he's like, "Holy shit, Batman!" Plasmas. Rolex! Fuckin' bling-a-ling diamonds all over the place. They say, "Go. Dump this out on bitch-ass Earth." 'Cause alien planet gots too much gold in it, know what I'm saying? He's like, "Uh, OK." So he takes their trash to his trash rocket. At first he's all worrying 'bout what they gonna do to him when he comes *back* landin' on Earth. But then *money* starts falling straight from the sky. People are all cheering. Dancing in

the streets. Everybody collecting paychecks from nothing.
No more unemployment Big Mac breakfasts. Name him
Prince of the Earth. Welcome back, Homecoming King.
Strippers all stripping for free 'cause there ain't no need for
money no more. *Alien. Trash. Man.*

THE RELEASE OF A LIVE PERFORMANCE
Sherry Kramer

Seriocomic
SCOTT, late 20s to early 30s

SCOTT *is an asshole—at least he is tonight. He thinks he's General Sherman, cutting a swatch across America, trying to drink every drop and sleep with every woman on his bachelor pilgrimage to the altar. He's wearing a cowboy hat and boots but he's no cowboy. He's an investment banker from Houston. The trucker who gave him a ride,* BRENT, *has just run for the bathroom after eating a 72-ounce steak in an hour, leaving* SCOTT *in a strange living room with a woman he doesn't recognize. But fate has brought him back to the town he grew up in and the woman,* COCO, *is the little girl who fell in love with him 20 years ago.*

SCOTT   [*Enters stumbling drunk. Sees* COCO *out cold on the floor.*]

Did he make it? See, Brent, I tole you you'd make it. Tole the ole boy he'd make it. And I'm gonna make it.

[*Singing.*]

"I'm getting married in the morning,
Ding dong, the bells are gonna chimmmmmeee" . . .

[*Goes over to* COCO, *squats down over her prone body, and speaks confidentially.*]

You ever notice the Freudian implications of that song? They're there all right. You start off—he's getting married in the morning. Now what, you say, what is so fuckin' ac-cordion Freudian about that? Well, I'll tell you. It's like this. It's like from the beginning of recorded time. You know the story of Abraham and Isaac? Everybody knows the story of Abraham and Isaac. Everybody knows God said, "Take him out and cut him open. Sacrifice him. To me." Everybody knows how it turned out. What they don't know is that God specifically specified for it to happen in the morning. God said, "Abe, babe, you gotta slip out early in the morning, before Sarah wakes up and sees you on the lam." On the lamb—

[*He "baaas" like a lamb.*]

. . . get it? "Sneak out before the bitch throws a monkey wrench," is what he probably said. 'Cause God was wise to the ways of women. Think he would have gotten a tumble if he'd asked Sarah to go out and take a kitchen knife to the joy of her old age? No Way. And so it has been, even unto this day. A man wants to go hunting, fishing—a man wants to do any of the things a man wants to do a woman doesn't want him to—he sneaks out to do it in the morning. I don't mind telling you, I insisted on a morning wedding. But it doesn't stop there. No sir.

"I'm getting married in the morning,
Ding dong, de dumdum dumdum daaaaa" . . .

. . . Dong, get it? Oh yeah, ding *dong* the bells are gonna *chime*. That's what happens, all right. Ring 'em and they chime. 'Cause ole Brent's gonna get me to the church on time.

[*He bends down and looks at COCO closely.*]

You look familiar. But that don't mean anything. You all look alike.

[*Looks at her some more.*]

Funny. From what Brent told me I figured you'd be taller. Allow me to introduce myself. I'm a buddy of ole Brent's—

picked me up outside of Houston. See, I'm hitching my way to get hitched. I'm getting married in the morning, see, so I'm hitching my way to get—aw, forget it.

ROSE (from The Hallway Trilogy)
Adam Rapp

Seriocomic
JERRY, 20s

JERRY, a slightly addled young man, is in love with a woman who lives in his apartment building. Here, he asks her sister MEGAN, who also lives in his building, if she has a clue as to why the woman he's crazy about won't give him the time of day.

JERRY   Why won't she marry me?! She won't even give me a chance! Is it because I'm not interested in playing bridge in East Hampton or spending weekends on the Jersey Shore with all of those rich fools?! Those withering lobsters parading around in their Coupe de Villes and Eldorados?! I'm an educated man, Megan. I went to Princeton University! I could have gone to medical school! I graduated magna cum laude. I choose to work in the subway tunnels—I choose to do that! To work among the common people is important to me! To work! That doesn't mean I don't have something to offer a woman! That doesn't mean a man doesn't have character or so much love in his heart it could burst! Your sister didn't even go to college! In fact, she can't even get a job as a secretary! You know how I know? Because I followed her to an interview at Sullivan and Cromwell last week. I walked all the way down to Broad Street. I watched her stop and feed the pigeons on the corner of Canal and Church. And I saw her buy a pretzel off a wagon two blocks later! And she went back to him for mustard and a napkin! And I saw her check her reflections in a window of a parked cab on Duane Street. I watched her all the way to Broad Street. I spied on your sister! I saved her life, Megan. I love her so much, Megan. From the moment she stumbled on the subway platform . . . I grabbed her around the waist . . . The express train rushing by . . . She gave herself to me . . . Right there in my arms. She surrendered. It was the smallest thing but I've never known anything more definite.

ROUNDELAY
R. N. Sandberg

Dramatic
GUPTA: 30s, East Indian

GUPTA *is speaking to* PRIYA. *Her father has arranged for* GUPTA *to marry her, but* GUPTA *has come to* PRIYA *to ask her himself.*

GUPTA   The ocean is one of the great joys of life they say. I beg your pardon. I did not mean to startle you, Priya. The ocean? To plunge in. Nothing holding you in place. Floating freely. Heaven! But America? It is overrated, you know. The romantic choice for the greedy. Make a fortune, they think. But India's the place to make one's fortune today. We have all the opportunity. That's why the Americans are coming to us. Though America's science is very good. Very good. If you want to cross the ocean, go to Africa. Yes, HIV/AIDS, I know. But not by the ocean, not on their beaches. Dar, Maputo, Durban—extraordinarily beautiful I'm told. I have family in Africa, you know. I've been saying I should visit them. It would be ideal for a special holiday. The kind a couple takes to celebrate their life together. Do you know what I say to my relatives whenever they tell me theirs is the most beautiful place in the world? Do you know, Priya? I say there is nothing more beautiful than what I gaze upon right here. In our little town, in our little clinic. What I see every day. The people with whom I work. The people for whom I care deeply. The people who bring me joy each and every moment of each and every day. And of course our wondrous lake. You know I am speaking about you. I am so pleased to be here with you, my Priya. So pleased. My heart would lie down at your feet if it could. It would kiss your lovely ankles and stroke your calves. No, no. Let me say what I have to say. I have come with a purpose. I think you know this. And though it is a joyous occasion, I struggle to express what I feel. Priya, our families are the oldest and most prominent in this town. We have grown up together, sharing everything in our lives. And these last three years with you beside me every day in clinic—when the end of work came each day and we returned to our own homes, our own beds, I said no, no this is not right. This is not what our lives were meant to be. Please. Just this one question. Allow me to ask and to hear your beautiful answer. I know I do not have to. Your father has spoken of the bond already. But it is your words I long to hear. Your heart against mine. Your soul and mine like the oceans of the world, separate in name but flowing together all as one in their physical incarnations.

ROUNDELAY
R. N. Sandberg

Dramatic
FRANCISCO: late teens, Latino

FRANCISCO is speaking to TONY. *FRANCISCO's a computer geek who works as a kind of hacker.* TONY's *come to* FRANCISCO *for help finding a woman he met online, but now has doubts about going through with it because* FRANCISCO, *who's young and not exactly professional, isn't what* TONY *expected.* FRANCISCO's *trying to convince* TONY *to let him do the job.*

FRANCISCO   I'm playing with you. You wanna find her, right? Real bad, right? I bet she's hot. She hot? She put her picture up? Fucking guarangas and shit? The flesh so ripe you can taste it? Come on, man, I'm shitting you. Bullshit boy talk, you know. But I can see that's not your game. You know how it is, right? You can't trust most of that cyber shit. Not that I wanna lose your business. People are fuckin' with each other all the time. It's old news. I can see you're straight, man. I mean full of the force, nothing on the dark side. People are good and all that shit. I can get down with that. She may be P Cruz with the heart of Mother Teresa and not give a shit about your wallet. Who knows? But look, you'll never know if you walk away, now. You have to do this, you said. So follow your heart now, man. It got you this far. It's only a little green. Find out what her deal is. It's gonna change your life one way or the other. Look, I can see you're a proper dude. Upstanding member of the community and all that. Your heart, your heart has been touched. Like never before. You can't think of anything else, not work, not food, not your friends. Your fingers touch the keys and it's like her skin ignites you. Your body quivers as the words fill the screen. It's like her soft breath brushes your cheek with each sentence. Flickering letters pulse with your chest. You want to kiss every word. You want to burn the screen into your body. There can't be anything between the two of you any more. Nothing. Just her and you together. And that's why you're here. We all need somebody, man. Let me help you. Let me put you together so the electricity that binds you is snappin' direct. No wires, no glass, no distance. Flesh to flesh. Soul to soul. One.

A RUSSIAN PLAY
Don Nigro

Dramatic
NIKOLAY, 31

NIKOLAY is a successful Russian novelist and playwright who has come to spend part of his summer at the Volkonsky estate in the Russian provinces. Here, in the gazebo on a summer day, he finds himself alone with ANYA, the youngest Volkonsky daughter, an innocent girl who loves art and the theater and desperately wants to become a writer. She admires him and his work with a deep passion that embarrasses him. He is not really a bad fellow at heart, but he's cynical, bored, knows that his work is superficial and worthless, and his self-absorption leads him to be oblivious of the fact that he is crushing this poor girl's hopes rather brutally. He really doesn't mean to. He just doesn't see it until it's too late.

NIKOLAY   I'll tell you what the theater is about. It's about people like you who are always wanting things, and trying to get things, and failing to get them, and suffering. And that's just the actors, but it's also true about the characters they play. Or they get what they want, and then suffer because they find they didn't want what they thought they wanted after all. Or they get what they want and then lose it and suffer some more. In a tragedy, we identify with the people who are suffering, although a good deal of the pleasure we get is because we're happy they're not us. In a comedy, on the other hand, we stand back and snarl at them and cough, and this mixture of snarling and coughing we call laughter, and tell ourselves it's a good thing, but it's not. Suffering is not a good thing—Dostoyevsky was an idiot—and laughter is not a good thing either, because laughter is cruel, and cruelty is not a good thing, because ultimately it's boring, like everything else. In the end it's all futility. Absolute folly and futility. If you want to write, fine—then write. It doesn't make a bit of difference one way or the other to me or anyone else on earth. Nobody really cares about anybody else's writing. Nobody can stop you from writing if you really can't help it. But if you imagine that it will make you happy, you're a fool. And if you think it will make anybody else happy, you're insane. What kind of jackass is made happy by Shakespeare? People dressing up in other people's clothing and then not recognizing each other? How stupid can these people be? Are they all cross-eyed? If anybody ever put on a pair of spectacles, half of those plays would be over in the first act. People strangling each other and cutting off their hands. Really. The theater is like a charnel house. It may seduce a person into caring about it for a while, but in the end, it's all rubbish, like everything else. All writing is rubbish. Even life and joy and hope aren't really life and joy and hope. They're actually death and suffering and despair as seen by an idiot. There, I've just come dangerously close to quoting Shakespeare—clear evidence that I haven't an original thought in my head. I'm usually more clever than this, but I haven't slept in weeks, and when I do finally nod off for a moment, I have horrendous nightmares about soup made of ox eyes, and the soup is looking at me. There's a perfect image of Russian art: ox eyes bobbing in the soup. Or I'm walking in a field of thick, sweet-smelling grass, and I come upon the skeleton of a horse, bleached white, and I see windmills turning in the distance, and suddenly I know that God is coming to kill me. I can feel him in the wind. That's what a writer's life is like. Eating soup that looks back at you and waiting in a field for God to come and kill you. [*Pause.*] I've disappointed you. Well, if you want to be a writer, get used to it.

SAMUEL J. AND K.
Mat Smart

Comic
J., 29

SAMUEL J. *tells his brother* SAMUEL K. *about a situation he encountered at the local Dunkin' Donuts.*

J.   I'm not ready for anything! I mean, I go to the Dunkin'
Donuts drive-thru on my way out to Lisle in the morning
and I'm never even ready to order. "May I take your order?"
Whoop—my mind goes blank. I know I'm hungry, but
do I want a doughnut, a muffin, or a breakfast sandwich?
And then what kind of doughnut?—what kind of muffin?
Sometimes I have to say, "You know what? I'm just gonna
park and come in." I was in there yesterday and there was
this guy complaining to the woman about how she cut his
bagel. He was like, "You never cut my bagel in half—it's
always like so-not-down-the-middle—how hard is it to cut
something down the middle?" And this like sixty-year-old
guy is going off and I'm just like—not in a rude voice, like
in a nice voice—nice-ish voice—"Dude, maybe you should
just make your own bagel at home and cut it the way you
want." He's like, "What'd you say to me?" I'm like, "She's got
ten people in line, it's a bagel, it's not worth getting upset
about." And he's like, "Mind your own business." And I was
like—in a not-so nice-ish voice—"Well, sir, it's people like
you that make the world a shitty place. It's people like you
that make me want to live on a deserted island." And he
was like, "Would you like to say that to me again outside?"
And then I was like—to this *sixty*-year-old dude—"Okay,
grandpa, let's do this!" But then the woman working there
was like, "Please gentlemen!—it's okay—I am happy to

cut the bagel any which way—it's my job—it's okay." And both me and the guy shut up. And I just stare at the floor. I wanted to go cry in my car, but I was like—if I leave now, how am I ever going to come back into the Dunkin' Donuts that is right on the way to the Arboretum?

A SEAGULL IN THE HAMPTONS
Emily Mann

Comic
ALEX, 19

ALEX's mother is a Famous Actress—a fact that he finds infinitely oppressive—particularly as he detests the theater . . . well, the kind of theater his mother loves. Here, he tells this to his uncle, his mother's brother.

ALEX   My mother hates me. I'm nineteen years old and a constant reminder to her that she's not thirty-two. Her whole life is the "theatuh!" And she knows I hate the theater. Not pure theater. I don't hate that. I hate her kind of theater! It's so fake! People marching around pretending like they're in some living room. I mean, all they do is talk and they're boring and pathetic and old . . . and they have nothing to say. I mean, who cares, really? The world is falling apart, or worse, the planet is dying! And these people go to the theater to be entertained by people who are just like them—or even worse, more clueless than they are! And because the producers are so concerned about not offending anybody while they pay their one hundred fucking dollars, there is nothing controversial or worthwhile going on. Unless, of course, it's from England! Then, of course, like good colonialists we bow down to their British accents—anything in British accents makes Americans feel inferior, especially in the theater—and we say it's brilliant, even when it's just—pretentious crap or little dramas with tiny little morals posing as great art—or those fucking cheerful musicals! Oh my God! I don't know. The whole New York theater scene makes me sick. We have to have a new kind of theater, that's all. Something vibrant, and young, and dangerous, and alive or, you know what? Just have nothing at all! *Why do we have to have theater*? I mean, I love my mother but she leads such—a stupid life! She dedicates every waking hour to something that just doesn't matter! And you can imagine how utterly revolting it feels to be me! Here I am at all her stupid parties full of celebrities and people who have all won prizes for something or other—you know, it's ridiculous! Pulitzers and Nobels, and book awards, and Oscars and Tonys and all that crap and here I am! I have nothing to say for myself; I can't even understand what they're talking about half the time; and they're all wondering how Maria could have spawned such a pathetic little loser.

SEX CURVE
Merridith Allen

Comic
JOSH, 25 to 30

JOSH's beautiful, brainy neighbor is a biochemist who has created a serum in order to control who a person falls in love with. Intrigued by the idea, JOSH offers to help MARISSA test out her serum in exchange for a business partnership. However, complications arise when MARISSA and JOSH begin to fall for each other, and finally, in this last scene, JOSH confesses his true feelings.

JOSH I'm it! I'm the reason Marissa's success rate is so low! You see, professors, Marissa developed a chemical substance meant to be used just by women. It was supposed to block the release of the oxytocin hormone so a woman could experience free will in terms of picking her partners. It also works on homosexual men. At least, it did work on her and her test subjects in the beginning. Until me. I asked Marissa to be a part of her experiment. I was the one straight guy involved in all of this. So she had to alter her serum to fit my biological needs. And while she was distracted with that, she didn't realize what was really happening. The charming effects of her serum began to wear off on her and the rest of her test subjects. And then everything started unraveling. So you see, because of me, Marissa was delayed in finding the right results and solution for her experiment. Now I'm not a scientist, or any other kind of expert, but I happen to have a pretty good memory. I see something, I remember it. And based on what I saw with Marissa's project, I think she should revisit what happened; look at every detail over and over until she can find another way to attack the problem. Because the serum didn't work for me, either. I'm afraid I fell in love, and nothing about this experiment could stop that.

SEX LIVES OF OUR PARENTS
Michael Mitnick

Comic
ELLIOT, 20s

Earlier. ELLIOT *has seen his ex-girlfriend,* HANNAH, *making out with a stranger in a bar. Imbued with courage (and possibly alcohol), he calls her and tells her off.*

ELLIOT   And when I saw you, with . . . with your arms around that . . . guy, I wanted to kill myself. God, Hannah, I mean, he wasn't even that attractive. I could only see the back of his head, but I've seen better backs of heads. Still, guess what, Hannah? Guess what? You make this really annoying noise when you lick yogurt off a spoon. [*He imitates the sound four or five times.*] You broke my heart . . . Hey ya know what, Hannah . . . I hate that dumb tattoo you got on your right shoulder. "A for Anarchy." I know I told you it was cool, but it's actually pretty friggin' stupid. What kind of anarchist makes custom jewelry? You went to Mount Holyoke for Christ's sake. Your dad pays your VISA. But what I'm callin' to say is . . . Hannah . . . Someone can like me. Someone can find me attractive. Someone can actually want to be with me. It doesn't always have to be the other way around. So . . . in conclusion, bend over, fuck yourself in the dick and I wish you my best. My number's the same if you want to call me back. [*He ends the call and smiles.*]

SHOW US YER TATS
Kent Thompson

Seriocomic
DOG, 32

Recently fired undercover cop BAD DOG (DOUG) *is speaking to*
LEON. DOG *has beaten up a man he caught robbing his apart-
ment, and* DOG'*s wife has left him, probably for another woman.
The police department is squeezing* DOG *out of his pension.*

DOG   So what happened was, I walked into my apartment,
and the first thing I thought was, Jeeze! Somebody's here!
And the first thought was *of course* Marcie. What the fuck is
Marcie doing here, I thought to myself, and walked into the
bedroom—and there the sonuvabitch was, going through
my drawers. And the first thought was that he's looking
for Marcie's panties because that's what guys do, eh? They
break in and the first thing they steal are the underpants,
then the stereo, the TV and stuff. But *of course* none of her
stuff is there anymore, which *of course* pisses me off, and
this guy is standing there with his face hanging out and a
pair of my socks in each hand. He looks like a right idiot.
Now, here's the funny thing. I level my gun at him and say,
"Freeze!" and he does, and then I go up to him and start
hitting him with the gun barrel because I am so pissed off
that he's got his dirty hand in Marcie's panties which aren't
there anymore and in fact were someplace else when she
was still around. Then I kick him in the shins because I am
so pissed off and kick his Jesus feet right out from under
him and he's down on the floor and I put the boots to him:
Wham! Wham! Right in his nuts. Wham! I kick him in the
face, I break his jaw, I kick him in the nose, break his nose.
He's a total mess, and I wipe his blood off the toe of my

boot on his shirt. And it's amazing—he never lets go of my socks. It really pissed me off and he wouldn't let go of my socks. So I grab another pair of socks and shove them in his mouth and kick him out the door and down the stairs. It's all a matter of timing, you know? Say he'd robbed me before Marcie left and I'd caught him. I wouldn't have been so pissed off and he'd just have been arrested and charged. He wouldn't have got the broken nose and broken jaw and miscellaneous lacerations. [*Pause.*] A man without a woman is mean, eh? He's still got my socks in his hands when he's out on the street and runs into a couple of uniforms who *of course* want to help him—he's such a bloody mess. He *of course* immediately confesses to stealing my fucking socks.

THE SNOW GEESE
Sharr White

Dramatic
ARNIE, late teens

ARNIE *has been trying to make his mother understand that his recently deceased father has squandered the family fortune and that now they are left with nothing but debts. She has said she knows all about it. He responds, with the rest of the family present.*

ARNIE   Do tell! Because this is the first *I've* heard of it! I mean—granted—something's apparently very wrong with me, seeing as I do everything I can, everything you ask of me, and still it's like I'm this, this . . . *bruise* . . . around here, as if I'm some deaf and dumb idiot who can't figure out what language you're speaking! I just for once want us to say what we mean instead of speaking in all this, this . . . old-fashioned . . . *code* language—it is, it's complete *Victoriana*, mother. *I* don't know what you're aware of or what you're not! I mean we drove father's body all the way down to Syracuse with O'Neil between us and you made nothing but small talk the whole way. This was *after* I telephoned the funeral director down there who said he was terribly sorry but he'd want cash payment in advance to service our family, and he wouldn't make the trip up *here* without it, and anyway the family plot had been transferred to a Mr. Thom Rathbone two years ago. Well what the hell could all *that* mean? But there we are with dad trussed up and practically bouncing out of the back of the truck and allll she can talk about is the poor state of the road, and gosh she hoped the weather would cooperate for the service. And after that? We get to the bank. And Mr. Fillmore says he's sorry but he can't give us any cash for the preparations because—for one thing—father'd exhausted his line of credit in June. Line of credit? And for another thing, the bank had stopped honoring his checks in August, and there were several dozen creditors who were threatening action. I mean it was as if . . . I don't know what. As if I'd stepped outside to find the sky was green. Yet after *that*, mother made chirpy conversation on the way over to the house about the amount of black crepe in the attic and how she hoped there was enough to fit out a more fashionable mourning dress. Never a word about the fact that dad's body's in the truck and somehow he hasn't left enough money behind to buy so much as a coffin, let alone throw a proper service. And then! Thom Rathbone himself, new owner of the family burial plot, along with Julius Whoever—that fat friend of father's with the bulging left eye—come to the front door with bad checks in their hands—dad's not even stiff yet, those sons-of-bitches—and she—this was masterful—invites them in to have a drink, and so successfully does she small-talk them that they leave an hour later drunk and ashamed. And the kicker? Is that immediately afterwards she shouts up to O'Neil: wouldn't you know she's *just* remembered father's always spoken about a plain burial under the chestnut at the lodge. And do you know what we say to each other allllll the way back here? When just ten hours before I'd thought we were—all right, not wealthy— but at least solvent? Zero. Zee. Roe.

THE SNOW GEESE
Sharr White

Dramatic
ARNIE, late teens

ARNIE *has gone over his deceased father's books and has learned
that he has squandered the family fortune. He is explaining to the
family what has happened to them, and how it has all been some
sort of elaborate ruse to pamper his older brother* DUNCAN, *his
parents' favorite.*

ARNIE   The real story is that from the get-go he's betting his
principle on stocks. The bank panic of '90. All zeroes. And
then bang: here's the big one, ought-seven. Pretty much
cleans him out. Which is when he brings in the accountant,
who gobbles all the crumbs. For the last two years he was
borrowing against *this* place to keep us in cash. But it's
tapped out, spigot's turned off. And we haven't made a
bank payment in . . . I don't know. Months. I always won-
dered why they didn't send me to join you at school. But
now I realize they probably never had enough for both of
us, even before the panic. What's funny is that I think in
spite of father's reputation, we were probably living pretty
modestly—with mother, father, O'Neil, and just a cook or
so, usually. But about a week before you would come home
on break, all these maids would appear. And they'd open
the spare rooms, and the dustcovers would come off . . . I
mean I suppose it might've been fun for them to pull out all
the stops a few times a year. They didn't have to entertain.
Just the spring and autumn shooting parties. Much easier
to keep this . . . little world alive for you. And when you'd
leave? So would most of the staff. I honestly never thought
anything of it, that's just what happened. The world . . .

opened up . . . when you came home. I remember one year, you arrive and everybody's all lined up, and you step out of the car like you always do, like royalty, you know, and you . . . have this . . . new smile. It's true, you look up and give everyone this grin, and all these . . . teeth. Just . . . pop out of your face. And sort of light up the afternoon—speaking of the world opening up. I mean you must've just learned that smile, because it wasn't there when we'd seen you at Thanksgiving, you must've developed it for some new friend—or it was a girl, I guess—but all I knew was, they sure weren't teaching that smile to me at Syracuse Academy. And we went to some Christmas gala that night, and I, I . . . just . . . trailed behind you, watching you try that new smile out. Teaching yourself how to cut a swath through the crowds with it, like some . . . glowing sword. And every head seemed to turn to you as you walked past. And people put their faces together and admired you. But then a few days later? You left back to school, and the staff went away, and the world closed up again. I remember thinking *well wait a minute, did everybody just . . . forget about me? When do I get to learn that?* I'd stand in front of the mirror at night and practice how to smile like that. Try to make my muscles do what yours do. Say to myself . . . *I* can make the world open up. *I* can make love come to me. *I* can make the future . . . fall at my feet. I really pretty much hate you. [*Beat.*] Look, that's not true, Dunc, I actually for the most part . . . this sounds odd, but . . . I mean I'm kind of in awe of you. Of what you are. And *that's* what I hate.

SOUSEPAW
Jonathan A. Goldberg

Dramatic
WADDELL, early to mid-30s

RUBE WADDELL, a former star pitcher in the major leagues, has wrecked his career with drink but is sober now and hoping for a comeback. He has enticed a carnival performer, REPTILE GIRL, to come to his seedy hotel room for a special performance of her act. Here, he tells her what made him decide to change his life.

WADDELL   I was down near Memphis when this storm hit. I was sleeping in Fire Station 11. Storm was tearing houses apart but then the dam burst and the waters came. We pulled some boats together but in a tangle of weeds was these little boys. I dove in and got to them. They grabbed on to me and nearly drowned me. They was so scared they clawed onto my body as soon as I came close. I was handing them to the people in the boat—suddenly something pulled me under. Dragged to the mud and I looked down and I saw the drowned unsaveable angry dead pulling on. They asked why they had to die. Then they turned into snapping fish and turtles and snakes and gators. I realized how much of my life I wasn't using. How many of them would have had a better fuller life than me. How many of them could have built something or done anything but live as a drunk on the floor like a fire station dog. "But ain't I the best pitcher?" And they laughed a black burp at me that even underwater I could smell. And I decided to let them have me. To give in to the mud. I gave up. Just as I let go, a hand pulled me above the water. I guess I am a cork. They pulled me up—my mouth greedy as ever for air. Like a new baby. And that's what I was. Then I went to fucking sleep and woke up a few days later. There's a secret for you.

STARS AND BARMEN

Reina Hardy

Seriocomic
RUPERT, late 20s

RUPERT, *an astrophysics PhD student in a city where no one can see the stars, leaves his lonely post at a computer and explores the nightlife, gatecrashing parties and trying to get lucky. In this monologue, he strikes out with a succession of different women at different events.*

RUPERT   Hey. Wow. HEY. Great party. I feel outdressed by the crudités. I am Rupert, by the way. I'm an astrophysicist. I'm in the business of identifying large, bright, and interesting objects. I had to inspect you more closely. I'm not saying you're large. You're very proportionate. And shiny. It's fascinating. So I take it you're involved in earthquake relief? Cool. Excellent. Inspiring. Listen, I'd really love to take your picture. It's for sort of a project. A comparative survey of women I'm attracted to at parties. Yes, that does sound slightly strange. I can be slightly strange, fair enough. Would you like a candy cigarette? They're totally legal. Okay. L'Chaim! To Rebecca on the day of her womanhood. I mean, Rachel. Thank you! She looks very mature. Not that I care about that. I'm here for the older cousins, and maybe even some of the cool aunts. I am very open to cool aunts. They have all kinds of aunty experience . . .

[*He stares at something large and unusual.*]

What *is* that? I mean, it's a twenty-foot Pentakis dodecahedron made out of tinfoil, but what's it doing at a party? Is it trying to say, "Listen, this party is way beyond you. You do not understand this party. You could be having a transcendent experience here if you weren't a total and complete imposter." Not that you look like an imposter, you look very appropriate. Appropriate, yet approachable. You have one of those faces. You know, one of those faces where probably crazy people just start conversations with you on the bus out of nowhere? Yeah. Well, it's been nice talking to you.

THE STEADFAST
Mat Smart

Seriocomnic
KELLAR, late teens

KELLAR, *a marine, is trying to write a letter to his sweetheart. He asks a fellow marine—a woman—for help.*

KELLAR   It's just that I get nervous and I start talking and talking and I can't stop. It's how I work things out and I've been writing this letter over and over and over—to Lauren—and I just can't get it right. She's gonna get this letter and just barf everywhere—she'll be swimming in barf this letter will make her barf so much—

[KELLAR *crumples up the piece of paper and throws it. All is still, quiet throughout.*]

I mean, she is so mad at me. The last night before I left— I took her out to a really nice dinner at this really nice place—it was like French—well, kind of this French fusion place—it was awesome. It was twice as fancy as the place Lauren and I went to for prom. And I got her roses. And bought her this bracelet that was four hundred thirty-two bucks after tax—like if you take all the stuff I've bought for any girlfriend ever before and *combine* it all—it doesn't equal four hundred thirty-two bucks. So I give her this bracelet and I think she's gonna freak out like in those diamond commercials—even though this didn't have any diamonds—and be all, "I love you, I love you, every kiss begins with K"—or some shit—but she just starts *crying*. Like bawling. And for a moment I'm like—she's so happy she's crying! Awesome, right? Wrong. She thought it was gonna be a ring! And I'm like, "We're way too young to get married," and she's all, "You're going to war tomorrow and you think you're too young to get married?" And we left everything a total mess—I don't even know how we left things and so I'm trying to write this stupid letter to say—

[KELLAR *gets the crumpled-up letter and uncrumples it. He reads.*]

"Baby, just because I'm not ready to get married, doesn't mean I don't love you." Barf! She's gonna be swimming in barf. Do I just need to propose to her? Should I just write: "Lauren, will you marry me?"

[*He writes it.*]

Agh! That doesn't look right!

[KELLAR *crumples up the letter again.*]

I just wanted to get like a female perspective on it, Powell. What should I do, ma'am? You're always reading those letters. Thought maybe you could give me some pointers. Please.

SUNSET BABY
Dominique Morisseau

Dramatic
DAMON: early 30s, African American

DAMON, *a drug dealer and hustler, is talking to* NINA, *his girl-friend and partner in crime, who is the daughter of two famous radicals. Her mother is dead and her father, who just got out of prison, wants her letters. These may be quite valuable.* NINA *won't give them to him.* DAMON *wants her to hit him up for money for them, so they can escape the life they've been leading.* DJ *is* DAMON's *son, who lives with his mother.*

DAMON   DJ is safe with me, Nina. I make sure he's taken care of. Got people lookin' out for him. That's the best I can do, right now. And you safe with me, too. You are, Nina. I know you think I be tryin' to gas you, but that ain't it. I'm too old to be tryin' to play you. I'm too old for all of this. These streets ain't for neither one of us no more. I swear to God—if I see another pair of shoes over some telephone wires I'ma lose my fuckin' mind. Kids do that shit to be stupid now. Don't even have no significance no more. Never know what it means now. Used to know—that's a hot block. Used to know somebody got robbed for they sneaks. Now you never know. These kids play by some stupid rules. Codes and honor don't mean shit to them. Whose set is whose—don't matter. They runnin' 'round like a bunch of pawns on a chessboard and don't even know the shit ain't real. Don't even know it's all a game. Shootin' each other over whatever . . . not abiding by nobody's laws . . . 5-0 or the streets. They just reckless . . . and they're the new leaders of the corner game. To hell with that. They can have this shit cuz I can't do it, Nina. And I'm not gonna do it. I don't want this no more. I want you. That's it. You and me . . . and enough to know my son's alright. That's it. Nina, listen to me here. I'm tellin' you straight up. You can't hold onto this grudge for the rest of your life. Ashanti ain't live free, Nina. Ain't that what she always used to say? She don't know what free is . . . never did. But maybe . . . maybe she know it now. And you can let her go. Give them shits up. Give 'em to the man they was intended for. Maybe that's the peace she get. Nina, why's this gotta be hard? Why's you and me gotta be hard? It's simple. Let them pay you back. They took from you—a whole lotta years of trouble on your mind. A whole lotta nights of stress—for what? Cuz you had to hustle, that's what. Pay your way on your own and figure out how to survive. And that's you, baby. That's not them. You still here and alive and survivin' cuz of you. Cuz you a bad bitch. And when you runnin' off with me—it's nothin' we can't have I'ma take care of you. Give you the life you been dreamin' of.

SUNSET BABY
Dominique Morisseau

Dramatic
DAMON, early 30s

DAMON *is a petty thief and drug dealer. He is upset that he missed his son's birthday and wants reassurance from his girlfriend and partner in crime,* NINA, *that he isn't the lowlife scum his son's mother called him.*

DAMON He turned eight today. Eight years old. Eight years since I helped the doctor cut his cord. Eight birthdays and eight Chucky Cheese parties and eight candles on a fuckin' cake. Seven times I remembered. The eighth one . . . I fuckin' forgot. I could say Rene set me up with that one but fuck it. Does it matter? I could say she usually calls to tell me the plan . . . usually asks me to buy the cake or book the arcade or foot the bill. This time she let me bake. Planned everything behind my back. Didn't ask me for shit. Knew I'd forget. Had too much on my mind this time. She was countin' on that. Knew I was plannin' to move away with you. Started arguing with me again. Been broke up over two years and she still on that jealous shit. Wouldn't let me speak to DJ no time this whole week. Every day I call, she got it so he's too busy. "In the bath." "Doin' his homework." "Visiting his cousins." "Asleep in the bed." I let the shit roll off. Know we working these last few deals. Figure I can focus and then holler at my son when I'm outta this shit for good. See him with a clean conscious for once. And what the fuck I do? I forget his eighth birthday. Day he ain't never gettin' back. Not neither one of us. And I showed up to his party late. Shit was over. No present. No nothin'. And still he came and hugged me. Like I was the gift. I was the muh-fuckin' gift. [*Pause.*] I ain't never felt so unworthy. But that's my mans, right? Devoted son regardless of my bullshit. [*Pause.*] I wonder when he playin' this shit back later in life, will he remember I was late. Will he remember I forgot and showed up empty-handed? Or will he just remember I was there. Rene said I ain't shit. Ain't shit but a lowlife mutha-fucka. Ain't worth a damn as a man or a daddy. She prob-ably tellin' that shit to DJ too. [*Beat.*] I wonder how long 'til he believe it . . . [*Beat.*] You think I ain't shit, Nina?

THIS IS FICTION
Megan Hart

Dramatic
ED, early 30s

ED *is speaking to* AMY, *with whom he had a passionate three-night stand following their first meeting, after which she disappeared, taking his wallet with him. He has tracked her down to her childhood home in New Jersey, where she is in the process of breaking some very bad news to her family.*

ED   You don't have to look so surprised. You knew I'd come back. That's me, right?—the guy who comes back. I mean, I'm the guy who tracked you down—all the way to fucking NEW JERSEY, after you disappeared, with my WALLET. Yeah, I don't know if you heard, sir, but your daughter's a thief. It's really disappointing, you know. She seemed so . . . full of promise. I should have known. I'm a teacher, you know. Ninth-grade English. Now, those kids are full of promise—bright faces, deep trust funds. I used to think I was full of promise too, but then, I've never been a great judge of character. But your daughter . . . I think she's got something. Or at least she better, if she keeps going around like this. 'Cause this is a lot to put up with if not. So, okay—HUGE mistake to come here! No need to mention it—I'm pretty clear where I went wrong. Guess you're not the only one with some serious impulse control issues, HUH? But did you really have to use me as your buffer? Or—not even a buffer—more like one of those blow-up bumpers that line the gutters at a bowling alley—yeah. You know—just the thing you bounce off of on your way to wherever you're trying to get. Maybe next time, when you have some kind of major life-changing information to impart to your family, maybe don't rope your new friend into it. JUST A THOUGHT.

Amy, you haven't realized this yet, but MOST people are miserable. MOST people are terrified. You're not the only one. Look at your sister. Look at your dad—no offense. But they don't seem like happy-go-lucky folks to me. And clearly neither am I. But maybe if one time you didn't walk out on something when you got scared, you might actually end up as the exception to the rule. And wouldn't you be lucky. We're all a mess, Amy. So get over yourself.

THE TIGER AMONG US

Lauren Yee

Comic
PAO: 23, Asian (Hmong) American

PAO, *an Asian American, talks to a class of seventh graders about the Hmong people.*

PAO   Okay. So. My name's Pao. You can call me Mr. P. That's cool, too, if you want. Right, Ms. G? Okay. So. Hmong. Everyone, they wanna know what Hmong is. Everyone around here, they like, what the fuck—'scuse my mouth— But they like, fuck, it's cold up in here and we're freezing our asses off and there're all these tropical Asians show-ing up. And they're like, I thought we were all blond up in here. So I can tell you what Hmong is. But it's like real se-cret. Like I'ma kill you secret. No shit. Okay, so Hmong, we come from a bunch of different countries. We ain't got no, like, Hmong country . . . I don't know why. Guess 'cause no-body likes us. Which I get—I don't like me either, story of my life—And we're from all over. We're in China. And then fucking Chinese—no offense, nobody's Chinese?—Fuck-ing Chinese, they're like, fuck you. So we go down to Laos. And fucking Laos—or Laotians—They're also like, fuck you, and they try to kill us. BUT THEY CAN'T! 'Cause we're TROPICAL SURVIVORS! With the TIGERS and LIONS and flesh-eating MONKEYS! We hunt those dudes for breakfast. We eat tiger for breakfast! Tony the Tiger kind! 'Cause we're CIA motherfuckers! You ever hear this shit? About how the American government recruited Hmong guys to fight the Viet Kong for them, 'cause I guess Asian-on-Asian violence is cheaper. OH! And we eat snake. For the protein. We bite the shit out of them headfirst and swallow the whole thing up. They're like noodles to us: snake ramen. That's our Thanksgiving dinner. People're like, "Oh, yeah, turkey," And we're like, "Oh, yeah, snake." Naw, I'm just playing! We don't really eat snake.

THE TOTALITARIANS
Peter Sinn Nachtrieb

Dramatic
BEN, mid-20s

BEN, *a revolutionary, tells his doctor,* JEFFREY, *about a secret organization that is planning to take over Nebraska. He wants* JEFFREY *to join him in the resistance.*

BEN   I used to have an older brother! Billy. Billy The Bestest. Billy The Beefcake. Everyone wants to be Boyfriends with Billy. Quarterback, Eagle Scout, Mathelete. Total opposite of me. And everyone loved him, told him how amazing he was, gave him 20 percent off. And my mom licked his feet like they were made of salami, while I never even got to eat my favorite cereal other than that one time. And Billy loved his privilege. Started to believe he'd earned it, that he deserved things more than others. "Equality is what lazy people want, taintface. You could be just like me if you worked as hard as I do." And when I tried to inform him about the illusion of fairness, he punched me in the face. And that was only the beginning. Billy became a bully. Weakness and difference disgusted him so much he would beat the crap out of anybody who was, a.k.a. me. He *believed* he was enforcing the rightful order of things. And *they* just let it happen. Teachers, authorities, my shit parents. Impressed by his strength, his viciousness, the fear he could instill in the disenfranchised. He was offered a full scholarship to Yale. I had one friend growing up. Edgerton Lansing. A scrawny, quiet, translucent boy with a cleft palette and a smell. Billy beat him up so hard he almost died. And while Edgey was still in the ICU, Billy went around town boasting about what he had done to this kid. And that he did it because the kid was a "fag." Quite a few "fags" lived in our town. "Fags" who all held a quiet, simmering rage in their souls that had been intensifying for years, waiting for one injustice too many to blow the lid off the pot. Rage felt by Billy's little brother, a.k.a. me, who knew the exact dark alley his older brother took home at night from the Kwik Stop and knew precisely what online chat room to share that information. When they found Billy, his body was barely even a body. Pounded so flat you could do yoga on him. And I'm the reason it happened. That's when I knew I was an activist. That is what a community coming together can do. There is a very powerful and potent amount of rage out there, waiting to be tapped. All it takes is a little spark . . . boom. And even the most powerful forces on the planet will come crumbling down. That's what we're going to do.

TROPICAL HEAT
Rich Orloff

Comic
ERIC, 20s to 30s

Tropical Heat, set on a South Seas island during the 1920s, is an over-the-top comedy about a grandiose missionary who falls for women of easy virtue, and the others who frequent the island's only hotel and bar. ERIC *is an aspiring tormented artist who lacks both torment and the courage to paint. When he finally finishes his first painting, he admits to* POPS, *the hotel's owner, that neither the painting nor his life has turned out as planned.*

ERIC   Oh, who am I kidding? It's a terrible painting. The colors create neither the illusion of flesh nor an imaginative commentary on the essence of the body. Not only does the painting lack dimensionality, it doesn't compensate by providing the sort of creative perspective which bypasses literalism to provide hitherto unseen or unnoticed truths. The painting isn't even bland—it's lifeless, as if the painter felt neither the power of paint nor the awe of nature.

Oh God, oh God, for years I yearned to create, and now my biggest fear has come true: I have no talent! My mind questions if life is worth living. I'm finally consumed with pure, unendurable torment! But wait! *Wait!* Even though this is the darkest moment of my existence, as I let go of my lifelong dream, a thought begins shyly to take form . . . Yes. Yes . . . An incredible thought. Suddenly I feel a brilliant clarity about how I should spend my life. I will become . . . I will become . . . I am becoming . . . *a critic*. Suddenly my life has purpose! To become a critic! If I can't feel torment, at least I can bring torment to others! Oh, to wake up each morning ready to use my God-given gift of pointing out flaws that people might not otherwise notice. To mock and humiliate in a way that makes rejection entertaining. To dole out approval with such scarcity that anyone creative will yearn for a kind word from me. What other life could compare to that? Thank you, Pops. If you hadn't pushed me to paint this monstrosity, I would've never reached this moment. Whoever I become I owe to you. And by the way, you need to spruce this place up. It lacks conceptual unity, and it's drab. God, I love the sound of my own voice! Here I come, world; those with fragile egos should hide!

TWO-MAN KIDNAPPING RULE
Joseph Gallo

Seriocomic
VINCENT, late 20s

VINCENT *is trying to talk his heartbroken best friend,* JACK, *out of going to Texas to chase after his ex-fiancée.*

VINCENT   The love of your life . . . ? Jack . . . you get *three* great loves: First love. The one who got away. And the love of your life. She's the one who got away. If she was the love of your life, then your life is over. The love of your life is still out there somewhere waiting for you. You act like I don't know what I'm talking about here. Like I haven't been burned before . . . ? I was quasi-engaged once. Stacey . . . ? You move on. You kill the love. You say good-bye once and for all. It's only hard because you're the one who got dumped. She left you and now you're stuck like Wednesday, right in the middle. You can't move ahead. You can't move back. And so now you're destined to spend hours of worthless energy obsessing about what you can't have. I mean I could smack you every morning in the head with a two-by-four labeled SHE'S GONE AND IT'S OVER—and *still* it wouldn't make a lick of difference. And do you want to know why? Because the heart will kick the brain's ass every time. Even if the brain's message is, "You two weren't meant for each other." I repeat, "You two weren't meant for each other." What I should have done is told you the truth the first time. Right before you got engaged, you asked me, "Do you think I should get married?" And I said, "Why are you getting married?" And you said, "Well . . . I think it's time." And then we had some bullshit conversation. The truth is anyone who ever says they're getting married because "it's time" is destined for disaster. The only right answer to "Why are you getting married?" is, "Because I'm in love." [*Pause.*] So stop acting like such a jellyfish and move on.

THE UNAVOIDABLE DISAPPEARANCE OF TOM DURNIN

Steven Levenson

Dramatic
JAMES, 26

JAMES tells KATIE, a woman he has just started dating, about ADDISON, his girlfriend, who left him. We find out later that JAMES, like his father, is a chronic liar. In fact, ADDISON was his wife.

JAMES   No, it's fine. It's just . . . Huh. Well. To make a long story short, I guess, she met—Addison, her name was Addison, *is* Addison, she didn't die or anything—she met someone else, a guy at work, she worked at J. Crew, and so did he. They had the same shift, apparently. And she fell in love with him, I guess, is essentially, that's the basic story. She fell in love, and she told me about it. And she told me they were moving to Portland, Oregon, which she'd never even been to. I'd been there, and I told her it wasn't that great. It rains a lot. Not as much as Seattle or something like that, but enough. And she has issues with, when it's winter and the days are shorter, she gets depressed. So I told her that Portland would just be the worst for that. It would really be a bad decision, purely just, objectively speaking, mental health–wise. So I told her that. And that I loved her. I was in love with her, still. I thought we had a real sort of, a future. And she told me, thank you, that was nice. She loved me, too. In a way, in a certain way. But not the way she loved Van—that was the guy's name, Van. So she was sorry, and she appreciated what I said about the rain and the winter, but it didn't matter to her. As long as she was in love. As long as she was happy. And then she, uh . . . then she left.

THE UNAVOIDABLE DISAPPEARANCE OF TOM DURNIN

Steven Levenson

Dramatic
JAMES, 26

JAMES's father, TOM, has just been released from prison, where he did time for financial fraud. TOM has been trying to reconstitute his family, and his life. JAMES will have none of it, and lays into his father for the pain he has caused his family.

JAMES   You really, you actually believe that you're the victim here, don't you? You actually believe that. I had the FBI come to my dorm room. They took my car. They took my credit cards. They took the TV, they took the computer. And you weren't there. I had to get on a bus, book Mom into the Holiday Inn, she had three suitcases with everything she owned in them. She was going on and on about the unfairness, the political, it was all political, there was no evidence, it was a travesty, it was injustice. On and on and on. The whole night. She was shaking. Her whole body was shaking. And where were you, Dad? And Annie. Annie's six months' pregnant. Her three-year-old son is crying, he wants to know why his grandfather is on all the TV channels. She's having panic attacks every three hours, they need her to calm down, they think she's going to deliver the baby prematurely, she can't calm down, they want to give her drugs, she doesn't want drugs, she won't take drugs, she can't calm down. She doesn't know if her husband is going to have a job in the morning, because suddenly everybody who has anything to do with you, everybody who has ever so much as *met* you, suddenly everybody has become a suspect, because you are *toxic*.

UNPLUGGED IN

Brian Pracht

Comic
ZERO, 20s to 30s

ZERO *is talking to his roommate,* CHRIS, *and his roommate's girl-friend,* LEAH, *about this crazy event he saw on his way home.*

ZERO [*Setting it up like a joke.*]

Alright check it out: I'm walking home a couple blocks from here, and in the middle of an intersection are these two guys—a taxi driver and a clown. A clown—baggy polka-dot pants, fluffy red hair, big red nose—Bozo the Clown. The taxi rear-ended Bozo's car, which for the record is regular-sized, and Bozo's like, "I have two more payments left!" and the taxi driver's like, "Fuck you, you clown." They start pushing each other, and the dude riding in the taxi—stockbroker type: slicked hair, shined shoes—he gets out of the taxi and is like, "I have an important meeting at so and so," and the driver and clown are like, "Fuck you, money." So they're all shoving and what-not, when I swear to God, a second clown comes out of the car—his wife, 'cause she's like, "Let go of my husband, you motherfuckers!", and as she's walking toward them, she trips over her big red shoes, like it's an act, but it's not an act, and she bites it hard, man, she's bleeding, and the taxi driver and stockbroker are laughing at her, so Bozo punches the driver, and bride of Bozo kicks the broker in the dick. By now there's a sizeable crowd. Cars stop honking, people's heads are poking out of windows; time ceases to exist. The driver grabs for the clown's nose as the clown's strangling the driver with his suspenders; the wife's attacking the broker with her shoes while the broker's searching for his missing cufflink. The entire city block's begging for more.

[*Beat.*]

The wife clown goes to her trunk and takes out a tire iron, 'cause the trunk's open from the rear-ending, right? She starts beating the broker with it. Hard, like she's swinging for the fences. Again and again, until the broker stops moving, until she's sure he's dead. The block was silent. [*Pause.*] I tried to stop her. But I was so, stunned, so caught off guard, my brain couldn't talk right to my feet. And then it was over.

[*Beat.*]

I'm shuffling home, trying to make sense of what I just saw, when something miraculous happens. I get an idea. It came from that quiet voice inside you, you know? The one that tells you truths you hate to hear so you ignore it? Well, I couldn't ignore this, because the idea is so brilliant in its simplicity yet at the same time so impossible to fully conceive, it has to be inspired. Right now I'm more concerned about its execution. Ever since I was a kid, I've been told I'm capable of greatness, and I believe I am but, I'm still looking for what I'm *good* at, you know? Where I belong. Suddenly I have an idea, and the voice is linking it to events in my life and how they intersect and connect. As to how to get it done, and what it all means, I've been given only fragments, puzzle pieces, and a promise: put the pieces together, and when the enlightenment comes—seven days, man. In seven days I'll know how I fit in. In seven days the world as we know it will end.

WHEN JANUARY FEELS LIKE SUMMER
Cori Thomas

Dramatic
DEVAUN: 19, African American

DEVAUN *is speaking to his best friend,* JERON, *age 18, also African American. The two of them have decided to make signs that they will distribute, warning the neighborhood about a lecherous man they feel is dangerous to boys and men.*

DEVAUN   This is good what we doin', right Jeron? I mean how we warnin' people and shit. I want to . . . I want to . . . do something you know like them posters of Malcolm and Martin or Superman? And I wanna teach people wrong from right or somethin' like that. Not like in church, 'cause that shit is borin' and it last too long, and the singin' is wack, 'cause they ain't got no good tunes. But I do like it when Reverend Buford start to clear his throat three or four times in a row, like this.

[*Shows him.*]

And start walkin' back and forth, and speakin' forcible, and his shoulders start goin' up and down like this,

[*Shows him.*]

And he start swingin' one hand with his knees bended. "Yes ah." and the people in the church look like they froze up listenin'. That's what I like to see. How they can listen to that one man and he short and light skinned and plain till he open his mouth and start speaking forcible. Then it's like he a new man. Like he grew or somethin'. I study that shit, 'cause I like the idea. But it don't have to be in no church. It could be anywhere. I could just say somethin' in a corner in the street, and people will stop to listen and wave they hands 'cause in the moment they will be like feelin' the spirit of the lord or the mightiful. If I can figure out how you could get people to sit on a wood bench till they ass burn listening to me. That's when I know I will become a dude with wimmins lining up and down the block waitin' for me. I will walk down the street, and the birds will stop flyin' and hang in the sky and look down at me like this,

[*Shows him.*]

Cats, dogs, raccoons, and wimmins and everyone. Just lookin'. At me. Like this,

[*Shows him.*]

Like, this thing we doin' to protect the people from Lor-rance is helpful and important. It's a good thing, Jeron, I can feel it. Can't you? But truth is, I don't think he can really run in them shoes he wear. They got them pointed toes. Them shoes he wear look like they hurt. It's the principus of the thing. That's what it is. I'm looking for the beginning chance to show people the real meaning inside of me so they can say "Whaaat?" I just want to do something for the world to know that when we walk down the street and sidewalk, people don't think we invisible.

WHEN JANUARY FEELS LIKE SUMMER
Cori Thomas

Seriocomic
JERON: 18, African American

JERON is speaking to his best friend, DEVAUN, *age 19, also African American.* JERON *is very smart, but shy when it comes to talking to women—the opposite of* DEVAUN, *who is a womanizer but articulation challenged.*

JERON   I dial. She answer. I say, "Hi, is this Larissa Shang?" And that's another thing, that name you gave me is wrong. Larrisa Shang don't sound like Lucy Ming, Devaun. The woman's name is Lucy. So the shit was confusing right there at the jump point. She say, "Who?" I tell her I got the number from you. She say, "Yeh?" I say, "Yeh." She say, "My name is Lucy." I say, "Oh." I want to punch you in your mouth right then. She ax me how it feel to be on TV? I say, "It aiight." Then I hear some quiet silence so that I can hear her breathe over the phone. But I remember how you said to keep talkin' and put your interests up front and shit. So I ax her forcefully if she want to git wit me. She silent. I repeat it, "Do you want to git wit me?" She silent again. I repeat it a third time. "Do you want to git wit me?" That's when she say, "What do you mean?" So I say, "What do you mean, what do I mean?" She say, "What. do. you. mean?" In a real nasty tone, in a low-voice sound almost like a man. So I say, "I mean git wit me. To git. wit. me. Git it? You know about that right? If your Moms and Pops ain't git together, you and all human beings might not be born." So I repeat it one more time, 'cause I don't know if maybe she don't speak English good or she slow, I say, "Do. You. Want. To. Git. Wit. Me?" That's when Lucy Ming scream, "I'MA SEND SOMEONE

TO FUCK YOU UP!" in my ear so loud it vibrate like a bell was ringing inside my head. But I say to myself, well, at least I know she understand me. Shit! But instead, she hang the muthafuckin' phone up on me. And when I call back, she hang up soon as I said "Hello." And this right here is why I don't like to do this shit. Like callin' muthafuckin' punk ass wimmin and havin' to speak to them so they can talk so loud in your ears and shit. Auno how you can think it's worth it to have so many girlfriends and what have you. Who want to git wit a woman can scream so loud anyway. I say, give me my own money, give me my own time. Wimmin is stupid. Some of em git pregnant and you gotta spend alla your lil money on Pampers. Then some of em want for you to pay for them to do they nails every week and shit. Why I want to spend my money on they nails? For what? I got more important things in the world to think about. I don't need to be talkin' on no phone to no stupid ass punk ass Lucy Ming. That's on you, telling me some lie on her. That girl ain't interested in me. And you made me call her like a damn stupid ass fool. I oughta whup you, Devaun. I oughta whup your fuckin' ass.

THE WHY OVERHEAD
Adam Szymkowicz

Comic
NIGEL, 20s to 30s

NIGEL *shouts to his coworker* ANNIE, *who has just left the room. She has unsettled him, but does not seem particularly unsettled herself.*

NIGEL   You better run. You better be afraid of me. I am a man. I am a big man and I won't take this kind of insanity from a girl like you! I have scaled mountains. I have forged rivers. I have run in races. I built snow caves and spent the night in them. You hear me?! I jumped out of airplanes. I drove a motorcycle. I am very hairy. I work out two or three times a week. With free weights. I eat lots of vegetables. I am a fairly good pool player. Also pinochle. I could catch a tiger if I had the right equipment and enough time on my hands and if I was in the vicinity of tigers. I have a charming per-sonality. I can make up jokes that people repeat later and don't even realize they're mine. I can make intricate cages out of popsicle sticks. My chest is enormous! I am a wealth of knowledge about music and musicians, especially in the years nineteen fifty nine to nineteen ninety-four. I write poetry. I won an award once for punctuality. My smile is terrific. I used to be a choirboy. I can peel oranges with great speed and dexterity. I am good at choosing shoes. I once played tennis for three hours. I am omnipotent! Okay, well maybe that last one isn't true. But I am a man and I will crush you. You hear me?! YOU HEAR ME?!!

THE WHY OVERHEAD
Adam Szymkowicz

Comic
DONALD, 20s to 40s

DONALD *tells his plans to his formerly alive, now-deceased, taxi-dermied cat,* MITTENS.

DONALD   Mittens? I finished it finally. My manifesto. You want to hear it? Oh good. I was hoping you'd want to hear it. Are you ready? Are you comfortable? "Manifesto to leave behind after everything has happened to explain why in case it is less than obvious." Is that title too long? . . . Yeah, I don't think so either.

[DONALD *clears his throat.*]

"There are certain times in history when certain actions become necessary. Right now it is a time when there are great inequalities. I have taken on the responsibility to right wrongs to stop injustice and to use the pen here and later the sword so that the words from my pen will be read. Anyone can write anything, but you also have to get people to read what you write. That's what the sword is for. I stand before you a man ready to take drastic actions. There are men that take actions and men that do nothing but complain. We are all angry but only the brave few who stand up and fight back will be able to accomplish anything of note. History will show that my actions were the right actions at the right time. History will record today as the turning point for America when a wave of citizens led by me took back their country. I ask that in my absence, one of my future followers take care of my cat Mittens. She needs neither food nor water. She has evolved beyond life. She only requires company and for someone to talk to her and listen to her. I know that Mittens and I will see each other in the next life, and I wouldn't be surprised if she became a conduit for my messages from beyond the grave. In the past, I have spoken to many great leaders through her. Like Marie Antoinette, John Adams, Martin Van Buren, Henry Ford, and a spirit guide dog named Hamish. So when you need to reach me, ask Mittens nicely and I'm sure she will oblige. And through her I will give you future guidance on how to overthrow the government and corporations and create a civilization for the people by the people. The right people, that is. In conclusion, when statues of me are built, I ask that Mittens be portrayed as well in bronze or gold or whatever. Her guidance has been incredibly helpful and without her I couldn't have accomplished what my actions accomplished. Like the straw that breaks the camel's back, the small deeds of today will reverberate for generations. I sign this with my left hand though I am right-handed." And then I signed it. Do you like it?

WHY WE LEFT BROOKLYN
or THE DINNER PARTY PLAY
Matt Freeman

Seriocomic
CHARLIE, 34

CHARLIE *is attending a farewell dinner party for his best friend. During the party, he attempts to explain why he doesn't try yoga to a particularly insistent friend.*

CHARLIE I can't move my knees more than 90 degrees. I had bone spurs all over my body when I was a kid. My knees looked like someone had smashed them with a hammer. Got them all shaved off, in a really painful procedure, between my freshman and sophomore years in college. Shaved bone right off my knees, my shoulders, my back. There are some little scars, but it's hard to tell. Even so, I still can't do a lot of things. Like sit Indian style. Honestly, it was this crazy situation because, like, imagine that you're already thirteen and you have zits and you're skinny and you're in Minnetonka, Minnesota. Everything is a fucking pool party or a party on a boat. Everyone wants you to go out with your shorts or with your shirt off and cook brats or whatever. That's the thing, like most of the year it's freezing and the weather in dangerous, and the rest of the time, around the lake, it's like we're living on the beach. So I would go through all these weird, I mean weird, twisted lies to avoid showing up anywhere in a bathing suit. Machinations. Elaborate scams. Invent funerals, killing off lots of imaginary cousins and uncles. I literally got in a car and drove home once, just disappeared from a party, because I was at this girl's house and they gave me her brother's bathing suit when I told them I forgot mine at home. I was in the bathroom, holding these shorts, trapped like an animal. I thought, "Fuck it, there's no way out." Drove away, just to keep people from seeing my actual body. So, I don't know, lots of kinds of exercise, that rely on flexibility, are challenging for me. Painful.

WHY WE LEFT BROOKLYN or THE DINNER PARTY PLAY
Matt Freeman

Seriocomic
JASON, early 30s

JASON *is hosting a farewell dinner party with friends in Brooklyn. In order to explain his dislike for the word "fresh," he recounts a trip he took with an old girlfriend.*

JASON   When I was dating Karen and we drove out to Pennsylvania to visit my mom. Karen was from, you know, northern New Jersey and had weird ideas about why some people got rich and others didn't. She was one of those people who believed that wealth and brains and hard work were in direct correlation, even though her dad ran a sweatshop and my mom taught other people's kids. I guess managing a sweatshop is like, harder work. We stopped at this one diner and the food was fucking Pennsylvania diner food. Normal, unimpressive, stock food. We were thinking about dessert, and then Karen asks the waitress about the pie. She's like, "I'm thinking about getting a slice of that pie." The waitress looks at her like, "Uh huh." So Karen's like, "Is it . . . good?" The waitress is this fucking who-knows-how-many-times-over young mother who is just waiting for Karen to pick "pie" or "no pie." Karen's like, "Is it *fresh*?" The waitress clearly continues to not care. Finally Karen, looking totally out of her depth, says, "*Sell* me this pie." As if the waitress is not doing her job properly, as if their status is not properly being accounted for in this situation. It's how she said it. It's how people *say* it. "Are those fresh tomatoes?" "Are those cherries fresh?" "Oh these peaches are so fresh." It's an indicator of a subtle goddamned palette. Demanding freshness is just a code for a belief that you deserve the best, accept only the best. It's a nose-in-the-air word. You might as well walk into someone else's house and say, "What's that smell?"

WILD

Crystal Skillman

Dramatic
JORDY, 19

JORDY, *a neurotic guy from Kansas interning to be a stockbroker and who is desperate in his search for any kind of love in his life, finds himself alone on a beach late at night with* BOBBY, *who he's been flirting with in the office.*

JORDY You have no idea what—I don't know what to do after Mesirow—I go home—when I go home and—I don't know what to tell them, you know? I'm pretty sure they're going to fire me. I've been pretty much wandering around the north conference room where they ring in Patty, all the people they fire on their fucking list—the meeting room where I put out coffee and I hear them deciding who is on their firing list—the names—knowing that they're going to fire me. And then there's another internship next year and finishing college and I'm supposed to know this is what I want to do Bobby! And I have no idea what I'm looking for! Not a clue! Wherever I walk into—Pippin's sweating my balls off—anywhere—I walk in and it's packed and I can barely move with people but I'm looking for someone like me. Someone like me right, but everyone I look at they *know* what the fuck they want to do, where they want to go. And where do I go? Go to a club—Angels and Kings or Downtown Bar and even then, even with everyone trying to go home with someone there's some kind of drive—some kind of passion. I don't know what to do with mine. And I go home with someone. I always go home with someone. Girls, guys, I don't give a fuck. I'm fucking someone and I don't even know I'm there.

WILD

Crystal Skillman

Dramatic
PETER, 25

PETER, *a stockbroker whose father is dying and whose own infidel-ity has set a chain of events into motion, including his own lover* BOBBY *now cheating on him, is encouraged by* VIN, *a calm "zen-like" young college student, relaxing on the beach to share what's upsetting him.*

PETER   My father. He's sick. He's really fucking sick. Sure you can say it's prostate cancer, but it's not even just one thing—drinking like—and his body is literally falling apart. Has been. Piece by piece. Not that he gives a shit. When I brought Bobby home? I didn't prepare them. We just walked in. As if we could walk in and everything would be okay. Bobby has no idea—he's just like, "They're shit, forget them!" Bobby's family they're—they love him. Bobby's mom and dad, his brother Ted, rally around him like— and mine? My sister Ellen tells me I'm going to hell. She doesn't say those words but she leaves reports of misery on my phone. Sends photos of dear old dying dad. Today's message? "This is it." So I fucking have patience. I get it together. I take my lunch break. I go to the hospital. I can't get past the doors. I look at them and other people going in and out and I know I'm on some list—like "don't let him in" but I know if I *wanted* to—if I *want*—they couldn't stop me—but it's me—I can't go in there—me—so—so—here's the thing—if you asked my family to cut me up and said to my fucked-up dying father what part of your son do you like? What one fucking thing of your son—what redeem-ing quality do you love? He wouldn't pick any part of me.

They wouldn't pick any part of me. I hurt them because of who I am. I hurt Bobby—I fucked someone else. A woman. I don't know why. I fucked it up. And I'm telling you this because I hurt people and I don't know why. I can't change what I did and I can't fix it. I'm just trying and it's not good enough. Not any piece of me is good enough and I don't know what to do.

WOOF
Y York

Dramatic
LJ: 30, African-American

There was a wild and raucous party at the stadium to celebrate the start of training camp for the reigning Super Bowl champions. At some point, LJ FREEMAN, their beloved quarterback, left the party and went to the field, where he was caught on a security camera committing a senseless crime. The video recording gets on TV news and the Internet, and by morning all of America has seen it and LJ is summarily banned from football. He tries to explain what happened to MRS. JONES, his revered but long-forgotten 5th-grade teacher.

LJ   I can't lift a desk, I can't even tie my shoes. I can't do any-thing. I don't know what to do. There's no place I can go. I ride around with yard guys. "Where we take you, Señor Freeman?" The only people talking to me are talking Span-ish. It wasn't a dog jumped on my back, it wasn't a big ol' dog, it was a Detroit Lion. Champion showed game films at the party—he thought it would be funny—a whole reel of me getting knocked on my ass. And there it is right in the middle of the funny film—the end of a nothing game, we're up three touchdowns, why am I still playing? Why am I still throwing passes? I drop back, and my offensive line—the most unbreakable line in the NFL—breaks, and a three hundred pound Detroit Lion flattens me. Pain—fire—his helmet in my back. The pain doesn't go away. I go to Dr. Scott cause I know he ain't gonna tell, he ain't gonna call the newspapers. He shoots me up so I can play. But the pain don't go. I play a whole season with fire in my back—but I throw, I always throw—It's me gets us to the Super

Bowl. The last drive of the biggest game of my life, my arm freezes, and I call draw plays—"He's a genius, he fools the defense," that's what everybody says—but I'm only handing off because my arm don't go forward! It don't go. All spring I'm sneaking to the East Side getting shot up with who knows what, but it don't go forward. And I'm supposed to start training camp, that's why they're having this party— everybody's there—all the gimme people, everybody with his hand in my pocket, helping me "celebrate" a new start. I'm the best quarterback in the league, except my arm don't go forward. How am I supposed to live without football? There's no money, there's nothing. The only way I have enough money is if I die.

PLAY SOURCES AND ACKNOWLEDGMENTS

To procure the entire text of a play, contact the rights holder.

ABOUT SPONTANEOUS COMBUSTION © 2012 by Sherry Kramer. Reprinted by permission the author. For performance rights, contact Sherry Kramer (skramer@bennington.edu).

AEROSOL DREAMS © 2013 by Nicole Pandolfo. Reprinted by permission of the author. For performance rights, contact Lawrence Harbison (LHarbison1@nyc.rr.com).

AFTER © 2011 by Chad Beckim. Reprinted by permission of the author. For performance rights, contact Chad Beckim (chadbeckim1@yahoo.com).

AMERICAN DUET © 2011 by Mark Leib. Reprinted by permission of the author. For performance rights, contact Mark Leib (meleib48@gmail.com).

APOSIOPESIS © 2013 by John P. McEneny. Reprinted by permission of the author. For performance rights, contact John P. McEneny (aslanbklyn@gmail.com). The entire text is contained in *The Best 10-Minute Plays 2013*, published by Smith and Kraus, Inc.

BABY PLAYS THE BANJO © 2012 by Kimberly Pau. Reprinted by permission of the author. For performance rights, contact Kimberly Pau (kimberlypau@gmail.com).

THE BAD GUYS © 2012 by Alena Smith. Reprinted by permission of Jack Tantleff, Paradigm Agency. For performance rights, contact Jack Tantleff (jtantleff@paradigmagency.com).

BARBARY FOX © 2009 by Don Nigro. Reprinted by permission of the author. For performance rights, contact Samuel French, Inc. (212-206-8990; www.samuelfrench.com).

BETHANY © 2013 by Laura Marks. Reprinted by permission of Jessica Amato, The Gersh Agency. For performance rights, contact Dramatists Play Service, 440 Park Ave. S., New York, NY 10016 (212-683-8960; www.dramatists.com). The play is also contained in *New Playwrights: The Best Plays 2013*, published by Smith and Kraus, Inc.

BLACKTOP SKY © 2012 by Christina Anderson. Reprinted by permission of Bruce Ostler, Bret Adams Ltd. For performance rights, contact Bruce Ostler (bostler@bretadamsltd.net).

BROKEN FENCES © 2011 by Stephen Simoncic. Reprinted by permission of Samara Harris Anderson, Robert H. Freedman Dramatic Agency. For performance rights, contact Samara Harris Anderson (rafanderson.39@gmail.com).

BRONX BOMBERS © 2013 by Eric Simonson. Reprinted by permission of Chris Till, Creative Artists Agency. For performance rights, contact Chris Till (ctill@caa.com).

CHARLES WINN SPEAKS © 2013 by C.S. Hanson. Reprinted by permission of the author. For performance rights, contact C.S. Hanson (cshansonplays@yahoo.com).

A COMMON MARTYR © 2013 by Michael Weems. Reprinted by permission of the author. For performance rights, contact Michael Weems (michaeltw721@gmail.com).

COMPLETENESS © 2011 by Itamar Moses. Reprinted by permission of Mark Subias, United Talent Agency. For performance rights, contact Samuel French, Inc. (212-206-8990; www.samuelfrench.com).